20 Gifts of Life

Bringing out the best in our kids, grandkids, and others we care about
(even if they're adults)

HAL URBAN

Great Lessons Press

Great Lessons Press

For information about special discounts on bulk purchases,
please contact Great Lessons Press:

650/366-0882 or halurban@halurban.com

Cover design and interior layout by
MacGraphics Services
Aurora, Colorado
www.MacGraphics.net

Printed in the United States of America by
McNaughton & Gunn, Inc.
Saline, Michigan
www.bookprinters.com

ISBN 978-0-9659684-2-3

For Jackie and Natalie,

Grandparents love to give their grandchildren gifts. They also love to teach their grandchildren things that will help them succeed in life. Sometimes these life lessons are the most valuable gifts we can give.

I hope and pray that these 20 gifts are the best ones you ever receive from me, and that they bring out the best in you both now and throughout your lives.

I love you,
Grampa

… There's something missing in the curriculum. We don't teach our students about life itself, about how it works, or about what's essential. Never has there been a greater need.

—From the introduction
Life's Greatest Lessons
1990

Our young people need more adults in their lives who model and teach what's essential—the values and positive character traits that lead to individual success and contribute to a more kind and caring society.

—B. David Brooks, Ph.D.
Psychologist/Educator
2012

We all teach, officially and unofficially, not only the classroom teacher or college professor addressing a group of students, but the experienced bookkeeper or factory worker passing tips on to the new arrival, because having an impact on another person, shaping his or her life in some small but vital way, is one of the most enduring satisfactions we will know. We teach because we need to share.

—Rabbi Harold Kushner

Table of Contents

If someone gave you this book

*A blessed companion is a book, a book that, fitly
chosen, is a life-long friend, a book that, at a touch,
pours its heart into our own.*

—Douglas Jerrold

Many years ago my best friend gave me one of the greatest gifts I've ever received. It was a book. He was moving away, and he wanted to leave me something that would have special meaning. When he gave it to me he said, "This book changed my life in the best way possible. I hope it does the same for you." He had already changed my life in the best way possible. He helped me discover a lot of goodness—in the world, in others, and in myself—that I'd never seen before. And the book he gave me continued what he had started.

My friend died in December 2008. I miss him. He was an inspiration to me for almost 40 years. The good thing is that he still inspires me, as does the book he gave me. I read from it often, and I think about him and what he taught me. Both he and the book continue to bring out the best in me, and will for the rest of my life.

The person who gave you this book may or may not be your best friend, but I can assure you that he or she cares deeply about you, wants to give you something that has special meaning, and wants to bring out the best in you. I hope both the book and the person who gave it to you will do just that for the rest of your life.

Foreword

I was delighted when Hal Urban asked me to write a foreword to *20 Gifts of Life*. One reason is that I'm a big fan of Hal's other books. I quote from them often in my own writing, use them in my college teaching, display them in our character education center at SUNY Cortland, and regularly recommend them to, and even give them to, people I know and work with—parents, teachers, colleagues, friends, and kids twelve and up. As I expected, *20 Gifts of Life*, like Hal's other books, is full of great quotations, inspiring stories, and practical wisdom that readers young and old can learn from and use to lead happier, more fulfilling lives.

Hal and I met soon after he had written his first book, *Life's Greatest Lessons*, published in 1990. It was selected by *Writers Digest* as Inspirational Book of the Year, and it became a best seller. Originally written for kids, it became popular with all age groups. In fact, our Center just gave it as a retirement gift to a colleague at our college.

Now, more than 20 years later, comes the sequel: *20 Gifts of Life*.

As Hal points out, the world that kids and adults live in today is different in many ways from the world that existed in 1990. In this new book, he applies age-old wisdom to changes that have had a big impact on our lives—changes in technology, popular culture (particularly TV, movies, music, and video games), social media, the influence of celebrities, personal finances, values, and the decline in civility and manners.

All of Hal's books have two central themes: good character and choices. Our character consists of our habits. Good choices form good habits; bad choices form bad habits. In the opening chapter of the book, Hal observes that "Good character is the foundation of a good life." Or as the Greek philosopher Heraclitus put it, "Character is destiny."

Because our character is the result of our choices, we can, at any point in our life, choose to improve our character. This is another basic theme of all of Hal's writing: Everyone's character is a "work in progress."

In our Center's character education work with high schools, we've had some kids say, "We've already formed our character by this age—we're not going to change." To counter this attitude, we've had students complete the following sentence, three times in a row: "I used to be . . . but now I am . . ." By doing this exercise, students can see that they often *have* changed, typically for the better—and that they have the capacity to continue to change in ways that will make them a better person.

A few years ago, *Newsweek* magazine ran a cover story on "the new virginity." It reported on the increasing number of young persons who, despite today's highly sexualized culture, are deciding to "wait until marriage." The article included accounts of students who regretted what they regarded as mistakes in this area of their lives and who were making a fresh start. Stories like these illustrate the truth that while we can't change the past, we can choose the future.

Or consider another example in the area of bullying, a challenge faced these days by nearly all schools. Deb Brown, a sixth-grade teacher-author that Hal and I both know, had a student named Drew. Near the end of the school year with Deb Brown he wrote: "I was a punk when I came to this school. I used to make little kids cry. I'm not a punk anymore because Mrs. Brown taught me character." Drew had learned to make different choices about how to treat other kids. Those choices changed the kind of person he was—his character.

My wife Judith and I recently read parts of *20 Gifts of Life* to two of our grandchildren while in the car on our way to a restaurant. It resulted in some meaningful discussion about both the joys and sorrows of life and about how those are affected by the choices we make. It was a good example of how enjoyable and enriching it is to read aloud and discuss—with our children, grandchildren, and other loved ones—a good book about living life well. Such is the book you hold in your hands.

Tom Lickona
Author, *Character Matters*

Introduction

Why the author felt a need to update *Life's Greatest Lessons*

In 1990 I took a year off from my teaching job to write a short, simple, and upbeat book about things that I thought would help our young people navigate life more effectively. I wrote it for a wide range of kids from about the fourth grade to those twenty-something's who were entering the real world for the first time. To me, anyone 30 years younger than me was a kid. And my greatest passion has always been teaching those kids things that will help them succeed in life.

The book was originally published as *20 Things I Want My Kids to Know*. It was a love letter to my three sons (then in their early 20s) and to my students, who were also "my kids." I knew young people wouldn't buy the book because they were buying CDs, video games, and other things that entertained them. But I was hopeful that parents, teachers, and mentors would buy it and pass on the lessons. I had no visions of grandeur about writing a million-seller and appearing on Oprah—which was good, because neither happened. I was just happy to get the book published (a tortuous process) and be able to touch a few lives beyond my own home and classroom.

The biggest surprise for this first-time, no-name author was the number of wonderful letters (this was back in the days before e-mail) I received from people of all ages and from all over the country. Those letters had two central themes: 1. People thanked me for getting "back to the ba-sics"—for reminding them about what really matters in life, and, 2. They urged me to give the book a new title because they didn't see it as one just for "kids."

Those letters touched my heart in a way that I can't de-scribe. A few of them brought tears to my eyes. A woman in Ohio told me that the book had become her "second Bible," that she kept the two together, and read from each daily. Then a few more people told me the same thing. I was hum-bled and overwhelmed. Others told me they found comfort, strength, and hope in the book. And many people told me that the book was a "classic." I don't write about this to brag, but to share my utter amazement at the effect my simple mes-sage for kids had on so many people of different ages and in different stages of life.

Because of these letters, especially those from business leaders who were buying copies for all of their employees, we needed to consider changing the title. The members of my publishing team were all in agreement that the word "kids" (one dear to my heart) needed to be taken off the cover. The reasoning was that they didn't want people to think that it was a parenting book or a children's book. It was actually both, but I understood, from a marketing standpoint, what they were saying, and I consented. The original subtitle had been "Passing on Life's Greatest Lessons," so we tweaked it a little. The book became known as *Life's Greatest Lessons: 20 Things That Matter.*

More than 20 years later the book is still doing well be-cause of the power of word-of-mouth. And I now get e-mails from people all over the world because it's been translated into several languages. The messages don't surprise me as much as before, but they still touch my heart. I strongly be-lieve that having a positive impact on another person is the greatest reward life offers. That's why I became a teacher, and it's the reason I continue to speak and write.

So if the book is still selling well (not to be interpreted as the author getting rich), and so many still consider it a classic, why would I feel a need to update it? How can you update common sense and wisdom that have been around for centuries? You can't, but you *can* apply them to a changing world. And that's what we live in. There have been more significant changes since I wrote *Life's Greatest Lessons* than during any 20-year period in history. As it was back in 1990, my goal is still to apply timeless truths to our current world in a short, common sense, and upbeat way.

And as it was back then, it's still my goal to write a book for kids of all ages. You'll note that not only the word "kids" is on the cover, but "grandkids" as well. But this time I'm aware from the onset that these pages are likely to affect adults as well. That's good, and I'll be honored again if that happens. I know a few people in their 40s and 50s who could benefit from some old-fashioned common sense and wisdom.

The only constant in life is . . . change

From this writer's perspective, these are some of the most significant changes that have taken place since 1990:

1. A new generation—Growing up in today's world is totally unlike the one we and our kids grew up in between the 1950s and the 1980s. Our young people know a lot more than we did, and this gives me hope. But they also have more choices and more pressure. So many of them feel the need to be connected 24/7, to multi-task, to do it all, and to have it all. They need our help in developing realistic expectations and in establishing solid priorities.

2. Popular culture—With the help of mind-boggling technology, it's become more influential than ever. I'm not saying it's all bad. In fact, much of it is wonderful. But there's also a dark side, and we face a greater challenge in helping our young people sort things out and helping them understand what's important and what's not important. The challenge to remind ourselves is almost as great.

3. Self-centeredness—Some sociologists believe it's at an all-time high. Our kids are growing up today with a constant barrage of messages that essentially tell them that life is all about "me, me, me." Unless they receive some help from wiser people in developing a different perspective, they're likely to grow up with a distorted view of life, unrealistic expectations, and a twisted set of values.

4. Incivility—Sadly, our world has become a less civil place. In part, it's due to the problem (me, me, me) described above. Overall, respect, manners, and consideration for others have been in steep decline for several years. One of our weekly news magazines did a cover story entitled, "In Your Face: Whatever Happened to Good Manners?" At the same time, bullying in our schools has reached an all-time high. I wrote a chapter about respect in my first book. I've written a chapter about kindness in this one. There's a need for both, but never has there been a greater need to be kind to one another, and to teach our young people to do the same.

5. A world full of promise—While we've experienced some negative trends in recent years, we also need to remind ourselves that this is a fantastic time to be alive! This isn't a book about doom and gloom. It's about inspiration and hope. I don't think society is collapsing. I see it, especially the young people in it, as full of indescribable potential. We're living in a world of unprecedented discovery, progress, and opportunity. It's more exciting, it contains more uncertainties, it has more challenges, and it holds more promise. All the more reason to be grounded in the basic lessons of life, and to draw from the timeless wisdom that's been handed down—and working—for thousands of years.

> The world does not require so much to be
> informed as to be reminded.
>
> —Hannah More

6. Grandchildren—Yet another significant change is the fact that the author and thousands of his readers now have grandchildren. Grandparents *love* to give their grandkids gifts. I want to give mine, and yours, the best gift possible: a little instruction book on how to live a good life.

7. The author—He has somehow managed to get 20 years older. And, he'd like to believe, wiser. He's also as optimistic as ever

Yes, some of the same lessons that are in *Life's Greatest Lessons* are also contained in this book. I think attitude, respect, hard work, honesty and the power of words are in all of my books. Teachers like to repeat themselves when they think something is really important. We call it reinforcement. I also frequently write and speak about choices, and you'll find an entire section dedicated to them here. But you'll also find several new topics that weren't covered in that first book. I didn't feel a need to write about them in 1990. I feel a strong need to write about them this time around.

A suggestion from the author

My wife Cathy and I discovered some years ago, while reading *The Purpose-Driven Life,* that reading a book together, one part at a time, and then discussing it, is one of the best ways to let the contents really sink in. We each had a copy, (this is not a sneaky attempt to double my sales) and read a chapter a day at a time that was convenient. Then we discussed it over the dinner table. Those discussions often continued afterward. So my suggestion is to read this book *with* the person you bought it for. Whether it's a quotation, a paragraph, a page, or a chapter, I think this is one of the most effective ways anyone can read a book. Read it together, and then discuss it. If you've never done this before, you'll be amazed at what happens. This doesn't mean, of course, that a person shouldn't read it on his or her own. I just think it's a better gift when the wisdom of the person who bought it comes with the book.

> *Books open doors of opportunity and help us see what's possible. They also glue us together.*
>
> —Samantha Avilar

A few comments on the "Personal Notes" pages

At the end of each chapter you'll find two lined pages under the heading "Personal Notes." I don't want to insult my readers by explaining what these pages are for. But I do want to briefly explain how they came to be, and to make a few more suggestions. We didn't include note pages in any of my previous books. One of my initial advisers and encouragers on this project was Sandy Swartz, a wonderful friend, educator, and grandmother in Wisconsin. We were discussing possibilities for a book like this while she was driving me through the beautiful dairy lands of her state. She talked excitedly about reading the book with her grandchildren, and then casually suggested, "You should put a few pages at the end of each chapter so parents, grandparents , and others can add a little of their own wisdom." It was a simple, yet brilliant, idea, and that's why the pages were added.

There are a lot of options for these extra pages: the person giving the book can write in them, the person receiving it can write in them, both can write in them, others can be asked to add their wisdom, and pages can be added, as Post-it notes come in all shapes and sizes. I hope you enjoy writing in the book and making it even more personal.

There are two ways to look at writing in books. One is that books are sacred, and should never be marked up in any form. The other, which is the author's position, is that if the book is your personal property, you can and should do anything with it that will help you learn from it. I have hundreds of books, some of them paperbacks that cost as little as 50 cents many years ago, that have yellow highlighting, red underlining, notes in the margins, and checkmarks all through them. They helped the first time through the books as well as the many times I revisit them. This is your book—use it in the way it helps you best.

> *I personally believe that there is no greater respect that can be shown a book than by using it. Do whatever you want with it to make it a lifelong friend and mentor.*
>
> —Jay R. Winger, Ph.D.

part 1

Five Lessons about How Life Works

> *I have a vision that by learning the laws of life and applying them to everyday situations, more and more people will find themselves leading joyous and useful lives.*
>
> —*John Marks Templeton*

There are some simple laws of life we learn as children. For example: if you touch something hot you'll get burned, if you eat too much candy you'll get a stomach ache, if you hit someone you'll get in trouble. We learn hundreds more of these as we grow older. They teach us that just about everything we do has a consequence.

Some people call them principles, or rules, of life. John Marks Templeton (1912-2008), the great financier and humanitarian quoted above, called them "laws of life." He wrote two wonderful books containing hundreds of them. I've always called them "life lessons." They help us understand life better and live it more fully.

In this first section are five of these lessons. They're about laying the foundation of a good life. I hope you learn them earlier than I did, but learning them at any age can, as Mr. Templeton wrote, help us be more joyous and useful.

chapter

1 *Good character is the foundation of a good life*

It is not education, accomplishments, material possessions, health, or significance. It is character that will sustain a child, an adult, a family.

—John and Susan Yates

Fame is fleeting; popularity an accident; riches take wings. Only one thing endures: character.

—Horace Greeley

The foundation of this book

Anyone who works in construction will tell us that the most important part of any good building, bridge, or other structure is a solid foundation—because everything else depends upon it. As an author and as an avid reader, I've come to the conclusion that the same is true of a good book. So great care went into the planning and laying of the foundation of this one. It consists of two words: good character. All the remaining chapters are built upon them.

With that foundation in mind, the two most important sentences in the book are the titles of the first two chapters. They're the two things the author would want you to most remember if someone asked, "What's that book about?" He hopes your answer would be, "It's about the importance of good character and how we reap what we sow." As you'll see in the next chapter, these two go together like milk goes with my morning Cheerios.

> Good character is more to be praised than outstanding talent. Most talents are, to some extent, a gift. Good character, by contrast, is not given to us. We have to build it piece by piece—by thought, choice, courage, and determination.
>
> —John Luther

Defining good character

Since good character is the most important term in this book, let's make sure we have a clear understanding of what it is. I spent a long time looking for the best possible definition. Many were written by brilliant scholars—developmental psychologists, experts on ethics and morality, theologians, philosophers, researchers, and some well-known writers. I found several more excellent definitions of good character written by schools and character education organizations throughout the U.S. and Canada.

And then I found the perfect one! While looking for something else, I found a folder I'd saved from a visit to Jacksonville Country Day School in Florida in 1998. It contained several items about the school, including its mission statement. I also found an outline from my presentation to the teachers, and some notes I'd taken while talking informally to a small group of fifth graders. At the top of the page I had written in large letters, "THIS IS A KEEPER!" Knowing that Character Education was at the core of the school's culture, I asked the kids to tell me what "good character" meant to them. Here's one of many outstanding answers I received that day:

> *I think good character means having a good attitude, always being polite, helping other people, taking good care of yourself, being honest, working hard, being a responsible citizen ... and not whining all the time.*
>
> *—Amanda, age 11*

Amanda hit the nail on the head like no intellectual possibly could. You'll find entire chapters here devoted to the character traits she mentioned. I loved the "not whining" part at the end, which came after a moment's hesitation. In fact, it made me laugh. Partly because it caught me by surprise, and partly because there's such a ring of truth to it. People with good character are so busy living constructive lives, they don't spend their lives whining.

Character and personality

It's also important to understand the difference between these two terms. They're often used as if they're the same, but are actually quite different. Although it's wonderful to be blessed with a charming personality, character is what determines the quality of our lives.

Character: The qualities that define who a person really is, especially when no one else is looking; the principles by which one lives; the ethics and morals of a person. No person is born with either good or bad character—it develops over time. Character is a choice, whether it's good or bad. Good character can be taught and learned, so a person can change his or her character at any time in life. Character can be chosen, taught, developed, and changed. It can also be faked, but not for long. Some people present themselves falsely for personal gain, but their true character is eventually exposed. A person's real character reveals what's on the inside.

Personality: The image one projects; how a person is perceived by others; how one interacts with others. Most people are either extroverts (outgoing) or introverts (withdrawn). All people are born with basic personality traits that remain constant. A few of these traits occasionally change due to significant life experiences. Basic personality traits aren't choices, and a person can't be taught to have a particular type of personality. Personality can be real or it can be phony. A charming person can be genuinely nice, or a charming person can be a fake, a con artist, and a thief. A person can be entertaining and pleasant in public, but malicious and cruel in private.

> *An attractive personality can be a great asset in life. Other people will like you, which is important. But if your character is fundamentally flawed, you'll never know the true meaning of success.*
>
> —*Stephen R. Covey*

What people of good character do

> *People of good character... act upon universal core ethical values.*
>
> —*The Character Education Partnership*

Earlier in this chapter I pointed out that there are several excellent definitions of good character. One of them comes from the above organization, often referred to as CEP, of which I've been a member for many years. It's primary purpose is to help schools and communities foster the social, emotional, and ethical development of our young people.

There are two key words in the partial definition above. The first one is *act*. In other words, good character is something a person *does*, not something a person believes in or talks about. The other word is *universal*. This teaches us that people who live in different parts of the world, are raised in different cultures, and have different religious beliefs, still agree on core values and what good character is. You can find hundreds of lists of what these universal values are, and you'll discover that they're all similar. To give you a more specific idea of what these lists include, you'll find this author's "Top Ten" list, in no particular order of importance, below. With each one you'll find three additional words that are closely related. All of them are universally respected.

The author's top ten character traits

1. **Kindness**—concern, respect, giving
2. **Honesty**—integrity, trustworthiness, sincerity
3. **Work**—effort, sacrifice, achievement
4. **Responsibility**—dependable, conscientious, loyal
5. **Self-control**—self-discipline, strength of mind, restraint
6. **Perseverance**—determination, willpower, purpose
7. **Compassion**—caring, empathy, forgiveness
8. **Courage**—bravery, fortitude, resilience
9. **Humility**—modesty, gentleness, calmness
10. **Joyfulness**—thankfulness, humor, laughter

A suggestion for your Personal Notes: You might want to write down the character traits you need to work on the most, and maybe even a plan for working on them. Also, get a few suggestions from people you respect. Are there character traits not listed here that you'd like to add?

Good character is hard work

*Good character is not formed in a week or a month.
It is created little by little, day by day. Protracted
and patient effort is needed to develop good
character.*

—Heraclitus, philosopher, 535-475 BC

Yes, developing good character is hard work. We don't inher-
it it, no one can give it to us, there's no "quick and easy" way
to get it, we can't buy it on eBay, and it doesn't happen naturally as we grow older. But please don't confuse hard work
with drudgery and unhappiness. Hard work is the joyful pur-
suit of something that's important. The happiest and wisest
people in the world are the ones who have worked hard at
developing their character.

Good character comes only from hard work over time,
whether one starts as an 8-year-old or as a 48-year old. We all
face challenges throughout life, from childhood through our
senior years. These challenges can also be viewed as opportunities to rise to the occasion, to be at our best. This is when
having that solid foundation of good character counts the
most. The harder we work at it, the greater the rewards will be.

*Our prayers are answered not when we are given
what we ask for, but when we are challenged to be
what we can be.*

—Mortimer Adler

A closing personal note

Good character is the subject of all of my books because I
have a genuine passion for it. Not because I've always had
it, but because I experienced what happens when you don't

have it. As I'll explain in more detail in the next chapter, I lost my moral compass in young adulthood and got off track for about ten years. Thank God, a great friend and mentor helped me get back on track. So I know first-hand the quality of life when good character is lacking and the quality of life when good character is one's highest priority.

The best news is that, no matter what our family background is, no matter what obstacles we face, and no matter what mistakes we've made, we all have the ability and potential to develop good character. We can strive for excellence at any age.

> *It is impossible to improve our individual lives or our society without genuinely caring about and striving to improve personal character.*
>
> *—Russell W. Gough*
>
> *Author,* ***Character Is Destiny***

PERSONAL NOTES

Personal Notes

chapter

2 *We reap what we sow*

You get back what you give out.
Those who do good do well.

—*John Marks Templeton*

Some ancient wisdom

Most kids (unless they were raised on a farm) have never heard of the words *reap* or *sow*. And not all adults are familiar with the words or the phrase either, so let's start with some simple definitions and a little history. The word *sow* means the same as *plant*. The word *reap* means the same as *harvest*. We harvest what we plant. If we plant tomato seeds, we'll later harvest tomatoes—not watermelons. Life works pretty much the same way. What we do with our lives, whether good or bad, will eventually come back to us.

Many people are aware that "We reap what we sow" is in the New Testament of the Bible. In fact, some can cite the specific book and verse, as in Galatians 6:7-8. Paul wrote, "A man's harvest in life will depend entirely on what he sows" (J. B. Phillips translation). This has two meanings: First, what we do in this life (good or bad) will eventually find its way back to us. Second, what we do in this life will also affect our eternal life. Please keep in mind that a central theme of the New Testament is preparation for the next life. You're free to believe only the first meaning or both of them. In the next verse (9) Paul advises us, "Let us not grow tired of doing good ..." Regardless of our spiritual beliefs, this is some of the wisest advice we'll ever receive. For the simple reason that this is the way life works.

While it's in the Bible, "We reap what we sow" actually dates back to a period more than a thousand years before Christ lived. It's ancient wisdom that comes from several of the Eastern religions and philosophies. This simple life principle was taught by leaders in Hinduism, Buddhism, Taoism, and Confucianism. It was considered by many to be a natural law of the universe, often called Karma or the Tao. The Taoists taught that a virtuous life puts us in harmony with nature. Buddha taught that good things will come to us as the result of right action. Confucius taught that morality, kindness, and sincerity lead to individual happiness and a peaceful society. Again, regardless of our spiritual beliefs, this is wisdom that can help us enrich our lives.

Also known for their wisdom were the famous Greek philosophers Socrates, Plato, and Aristotle (470-322 BC). Each of them wrote about the place of virtue and vice in our lives, and the results of each. Instead of calling it karma, they often referred to it as cause and effect. Aristotle may have summed up their teachings about it when he wrote that our actions will determine whether we will be happy or feel the reverse. We reap what we sow.

> *Our thoughts, deeds and words return to us sooner or later, with astounding accuracy.*
>
> —*Florence Shinn*

An important clarification

"We reap what we sow" is what John Marks Templeton calls a "natural law of life," and what the Tao calls "the way of the universe." It is, in fact, a basic principle that explains how things work in the real world. The more good we do, the more it comes back to us. If we're consistently kind, honest, and hard-working we'll eventually reap the rewards. On the other hand, the more bad we do, the more it will come back to us also. If we're consistently mean, dishonest, and lazy we'll eventually suffer the consequences.

But it's important to understand that "we reap what we sow" is a general rule of life. It helps us understand, as Mr. Templeton says at the beginning of this chapter, that we get back what we give out. This is true over time. However, we need to remember the old expression that tells us "there's an exception to every rule." "We reap what we sow" is not a hard-fast, iron-clad, rigid rule that applies to every life occurrence. Here are a few examples:

- A farmer can do all the right things when he plants his corn—prepare the soil, fertilize, water, weed, etc. But a tornado or a hungry pack of animals can wipe out his efforts.

- A person can take the best possible care of his physical health and still be stricken with a debilitating disease.

- A student can study extremely hard for an exam and still receive a poor grade.

- A whistle-blower in a corrupt company can do the right thing by reporting the wrongdoing she sees and still end up unemployed and scorned.

- Great men and women throughout history have courageously stood up for the right thing, but paid with their lives. A few examples are Joan of Arc, Abraham Lincoln, Mohandas Gandhi, Anne Frank, and Martin Luther King, Jr.

The crucial point is this: "We reap what we sow" must be looked at from a long-range perspective. The good we do over a period of time has a build-up effect. It *will* eventually come back to us, but not on every occasion. A dear friend who contributed much to the writing of this book helps clarify this point.

> We may not always reap a good harvest in the short run from the good that we sow, but ultimately, whether later in this life or in the next life (and this, of course, assumes a belief in an afterlife), we will indeed reap what we have sown.
>
> —*Thomas Lickona, Ph.D.*
> *Developmental psychologist*

What a schoolgirl most remembered

One of my favorite places to speak at is St. Peter's School in San Francisco. It's a small elementary school located about 25 miles north of my home in what's known as the Mission District, a mostly Hispanic blue-collar section of the city. There's a wonderful man named Fred Clark who spends a lot of volunteer time there. He teaches a course called Life 101: The Virtues and Habits You Need to Succeed in Life. If I were the King of Education, every kid in the country would take that course in elementary school, in junior high, in high school, and in college. Fred also invites me to speak to the kids, buys them each a copy of *Life's Greatest Lessons,* and provides scholarships for students who show a genuine desire to further their education.

I talk to the students about the seven choices we make daily that most determine the quality of our lives. There's a chapter devoted to each of them in Part 2 of this book. I love speaking to these kids because they have that boundless and wonderful energy that all kids seem to have. But also because they're so polite, so friendly, and so genuinely interested in learning more about life. Near the beginning of the presentation I tell them that before explaining the seven choices, I need to lay an important foundation. I then project a slide onto a screen that states in large letters:

> **WE REAP WHAT WE SOW**

Seeing some puzzled looks, I assured them that it was OK to not know what it means. I said, "That's why you're in school—to learn. And that's why I'm here today—to teach." None of them knew what *reap* or *sow* meant. Although one boy did think he knew what *sow* meant. He said, "That's what my mom does when I tear my clothes." I clarified that his mother *sews* his clothes rather than *sows* them, and then explained, as I did at the beginning of this chapter, the meaning and history of reaping and sowing throughout our lives. They assured me that they "got it," and I proceeded on to the seven choices.

In December 2010 I was delighted to accept yet another invitation to speak to the kids at St. Peter's. I arrived early so I could say hello to the devoted people on the staff there. When I went into the main office a teenage girl recognized me, smiled, and said, "Oh, you're Dr. Urban. You spoke to my graduating class a few years ago." She then graciously introduced herself as Gabriella. She was attending an outstanding high school in San Francisco, with the goal of becoming the first one in her family to go to college. I sometimes wonder what people remember from my talks a year or two later.

In fact, I often wonder if they remember anything from my talks a *day* or two later.

This seemed like a good time to find out, so I asked Gabriella, "Is there anything in particular that you remember from my talk that day?" Without a second's hesitation, she said, "We reap what we sow." I was pleased, and then asked, "Anything else?" Again without hesitation, she said, "I remember the story about Bruce (it's in Chapter 6), and I remember all seven of the choices." I can't describe how happy I was to learn that she had remembered so much a couple of years later.

I asked her to tell me why she thought of "We reap what we sow" first. She said, "Because that's what you started with, and it helped us understand how every choice we make in life has a consequence." I wanted to hug her, but for the moment, I was curious to learn more about what she remembered from the talk, and more important, whether it had made a difference in her life.

She assured me that "We reap what we sow" and the seven choices made a "huge" impact on her. Naturally, I asked, "How?"

She told me her story. Her family had come from Mexico and moved in with relatives in a tough neighborhood, one that was plagued with both high unemployment and crime rates. Her family was also poor. She had been thinking that college wasn't a possibility for her. In fact, she even wondered about high school. All of this changed when she met Mr. Clark, who convinced his students in Life 101 that if they formed the right virtues and turned them into habits, they could all succeed in life.

Examples of reaping and sowing — both good and bad

Gabriella also had a question for me. She asked, "Do you remember when you asked us to give you examples of reaping and sowing, both good and bad? That really helped us understand." Yes, I remembered vividly. Here are two more slides I showed before asking them to give me examples:

The more bad we do in life, the more it will come back to us	**The more good we do in life, the more it will come back to us**

Here are the examples they gave. They were so good—simple, yet profound—I decided then to use them in my next presentation. So I asked one of the teachers in attendance to write them down for me. Not only did these kids help me develop materials for my next presentation, they helped me write the second chapter of this book.

Bad sowing and reaping

1. **Sow**—Break the law: steal, do or sell drugs, hurt or kill someone
   Reap—Get in trouble and maybe end up in prison
2. **Sow**—Abuse your body: drugs, alcohol, tobacco, fat, sugar, no exercise
   Reap—Be fat, be unhealthy, be unhappy, die young
3. **Sow**—Be lazy: be a couch potato, do too much TV and video games
   Reap—Do poorly in school, achieve nothing in life
4. **Sow**—Be mean: put others down, gossip, bully, laugh at people
   Reap—Be disliked by others, be treated badly, end up lonely and unhappy
5. **Sow**—Be dishonest: lie, cheat, steal
   Reap—Bad reputation, not be trusted, ruin friendships

Good sowing and reaping

1. **Sow**—Obey the law: drive safely, play by the rules, do the right thing

   Reap—Stay out of trouble and be respected by others
2. **Sow**—Care for body: eat healthy, exercise, don't smoke, drink, do drugs

   Reap—Be healthy, look better, be happier, live longer
3. **Sow**—Work hard: study, help at home, be responsible

   Reap—Good grades, get into college, earn respect, be successful in career
4. **Sow**—Be nice: be polite, help others, say nice things, have good manners

   Reap—Be liked by others, be treated well, have lots of friends, be happy
5. **Sow**—Be honest: tell the truth, do what you know is right and fair

   Reap—Good reputation, be trusted, have good relationships

Talk about getting to the point! The more I looked at these later, the more I realized that these kids had come up with a concise and comprehensive plan for living a good life in less than ten minutes. Confucius said, "Life is really simple, but we insist on making it complicated." Thank you students of St. Peter's for simplifying life for us.

Learning from mistakes

I'll close with two examples of "reaping and sowing" from my own life. They'll help you understand why I'm so passionate about both this basic principle of life and the subject of the first chapter—good character.

1. Reaping and sowing the bad—I went through an incredibly painful period in my young adult life. Something both hurtful and unfair happened to me. Instead of getting help and learning to deal with it, I went into a ten-year funk. I turned my back on my faith and the values I'd been taught. I was angry, self-centered, insensitive to others, often rude and demanding, and frequently dishonest.

Not a nice picture, is it? And believe me, I reaped what I'd been sowing. Things went from bad to worse, and I finally hit bottom. Never had I been so lonely and unhappy. Pain is a great teacher, and it taught me that some major changes were in order.

2. Reaping and sowing the good—The turning point was when I received some wonderful advice from a man who became my first mentor. He urged me to return to my faith (and to learn more about it) and to those values I'd been taught in my youth. I followed his wise counsel. What happened? The anger dissipated, I became less self-centered (always a battle), worked hard at being sensitive to the needs and feelings of others, discovered that politeness gets better results than rudeness, and devoted myself to being a person of honesty and integrity.

Have I reaped the rewards? Absolutely! The rewards have been peace of mind, improved relationships, more friends, a better reputation, and a lot more joy. Does this mean nothing bad ever happens to me anymore? Absolutely not! During the three years that I worked on this book I've endured two of the most painful experiences of my life—one physical and one emotional. But as I wrote in *Life's Greatest Lessons* 20 years ago, "Life is hard, and not always fair." I've learned to both accept and deal with the pain life hands out to all of us (see Chapter 4). I've also learned that the more good I do, the more it comes back to me.

> *Life can be explained in one simple rule: we pretty much get out of it what we put into it. As someone once said, "We reap what we sow."*
>
> —*Kurt Ashbaugh*

Personal Notes

PERSONAL NOTES

---

chapter
3

Being smart means having self-control; it's the master skill of life

> *What factors are at play ... when people of high IQ flounder and those of modest IQ do surprisingly well? I would argue that the difference quite often lies in the abilities called here emotional intelligence, which include self-control, zeal and persistence, and the ability to motivate oneself.*
>
> —Daniel Goleman, Ph.D.

Growing up with a "brainy" friend

Most of the time when we describe someone as "intelligent" or as "really smart" or as "a genius," we mean that he or she is a lot brighter than the rest of us. This type of person usually finds school easy, gets good grades, and scores high on intelligence and college aptitude tests. Sometimes we wish we had their "brains." And sometimes we're glad we don't.

I grew up in a small town in northern California, and attended a Catholic elementary school from kindergarten through the eighth grade. One of my classmates during all those years was Alvin (not his real name). He was, by far, the smartest kid in the school. The teachers knew it, all the students knew it, and he knew it. We sometimes called him "Einstein." At other times we called him "The Brain." The problem was that he wasn't much fun to be around. He never laughed, wasn't very sociable, and thought games and sports were a waste of time. But he could sure do math problems!

My friends and I went on to the public high school in town, and Alvin went out of town to attend an exclusive prep school. He later went to an Ivy League college, and then on to a prestigious law school. Afterwards he returned home, and quickly became one of the most feared lawyers in town. Smart, smart, smart! He had very few friends, but made a fortune and lived in a mansion. Where is he today? He committed suicide several years ago. It turned out that he had been ripping off his clients for many years. The law closed in on him, he was indicted on several felony counts, and was headed for prison. He killed himself before the trial, and died in disgrace.

Why do I tell this story? Does this mean that all smart people who make a lot of money end up this way? Not at all. But it does show that there are different types of intelligence. Many of Alvin's classmates ended up with lower paying jobs, but raised happy families, still enjoy wonderful friendships, are respected in their communities, and are enjoying their retirement years today. They were "smart" in a different way.

Defining I. Q. and E. Q.

I. Q.—Intelligence Quotient. It's defined by Merriam-Webster as: "a score determined by one's performance on a standardized intelligence test relative to the average performance of others of the same age." Most people are familiar with the letters "I. Q." When we say someone has a high I. Q. we mean he or she is very smart. The average score is 100, so someone with an I. Q. of around 140 would be considered a genius. This may or may not lead to success in life, but it would certainly help to be that intelligent.

E. Q.—Emotional Quotient, also referred to as Emotional Intelligence. It's more difficult to define than I. Q., as it's not even found in Merriam-Webster.

The term "emotional intelligence" was first used in 1985 in a doctoral dissertation. It wasn't used again until two academic journal articles were published about it in 1990. The person who made the term famous is Daniel Goleman, Ph.D., when his best-selling book, *Emotional Intelligence*, was published in 1995. The subtitle is "Why it can matter more than IQ." Dr. Goleman gave us a new perspective on what it means to be smart.

He tells us that we basically have two minds:

> **Rational mind:** "the head"—We use it in school, at work, and in life. We use it to figure things out, to solve problems, to read, to write, to do any number of tasks which require mental processing.

> **Emotional mind:** "the heart"—We use it to manage, or control, our feelings (emotions) and impulses. We use it to know (in our hearts) what's right and what's wrong, to do the right thing, to understand and get along well with others, and to motivate ourselves.

Dr. Goleman explains that these two minds aren't entirely separate from each other. They both operate at the same time, and are interdependent. He points out that while IQ is better known and understood, it contributes to only about 20 percent of the factors that determine success in life. So 80 percent of those factors are determined by other forces. Emotional intelligence plays the biggest part, although the amount varies from person to person.

The six keys to emotional intelligence

Goleman and others in this field, sometimes called social-emotional intelligence, are in unanimous agreement that the skills which most lead to success are the following:

1. Self-awareness: This is a person's ability to understand his or her own feelings and moods as they're happening. Goleman calls it the "keystone" of emotional intelligence. It helps us to be in touch with our feelings, and to monitor them so we won't damage our lives.

2. Managing emotions: If we're aware of our strong emotions, then we know that we could do harm to others and/or to ourselves. This helps us to manage them in socially appropriate ways. An example is learning to soothe ourselves when we're angry. Rather than having an emotional outburst that we'll regret later, we develop a way to calm ourselves down. An example from my own life is explained later in this chapter.

3. Motivating oneself: Most people wait for something or someone else to motivate them. But people with emotional intelligence understand that real motivation comes from within. People who motivate themselves know that delayed gratification and perseverance are necessary to accomplish their goals.

4. Empathy: This is the ability to understand how other people feel—to put ourselves in their places when they're experiencing something that's charged with emotions. For instance, a friend loses a loved one. You put yourself in his/her position, and you "feel" for your friend. Goleman calls empathy the "fundamental people skill." People with empathy are more attuned to other people's feelings and needs, and more likely to be unselfish and caring.

5. Handling relationships: This is often referred to as "having good social skills." It means possessing the ability to deal with other people's feelings in a variety of situations. It's particularly important for people in positions of leadership to have these skills. Examples are teachers, pastors, executives, managers, coaches, caregivers, and administrators of all types.

6. Integrity: The word essentially means *complete*—all the parts have come together, or have integrated. Honesty is a major component of it (see Chapter 7). It's wonderful if we can control our emotions and impulses, develop empathy, get along with others, and motivate ourselves, but we still need to know right from wrong and consistently do the right thing.

Anger—the toughest emotion to manage

> *Anyone can become angry—that is easy. But to be angry with the right person, to the right degree, at the right time, for the right purpose, and in the right way—this is not easy.*
>
> *—Aristotle*

Most people who study human behavior agree that anger is the most destructive emotion, the one that leads to the most problems, and the one that results in the most pain. It's often related to some of the other destructive emotions such as hatred, rage, fury, and revenge. Anger is also the hardest emotion to control. Because we're born with different personalities and temperaments, some people struggle with it more than others. But no one fully escapes its wrath.

The author has first-hand experience with the struggle to overcome anger. In fact, in one of my prior books called *The 10 Commandments of Common Sense,* I devoted an entire chapter to it. It's called, "Don't let anger get out of control. It can wreck relationships and ruin lives." As a self-confessed and reformed "hothead," I know only too well the damage that anger can cause. In a book of this type and length, I can't possibly explain all the cures for anger management problems, but I can give you a painful example from my own life. There's hope for hotheads because anger *can* be controlled, and life is a lot more enjoyable when it is. For your own sake, and the sake of your friends and loved ones, get help if you need it in this area.

That's what I did—I sought help. In a fit of anger I once screamed cruel words at someone I deeply loved. One of the many problems with rage is that it prevents us from thinking rationally, so I wasn't aware that I was hurting someone I cared about. I wasn't thinking about the damage that words expressed in uncontrolled anger can do or how long it can last. Later, when I realized what I'd done, I was both ashamed and remorseful. I apologized profusely and sincerely, and was fortunately forgiven. But the guilt ran deep. I never wanted to make this mistake again, so for the first time in my life, I sought the help of a professional counselor. It was a life-changing decision.

One of the first things the counselor asked me was about my family background. Did I grow up in an atmosphere with a lot of anger in it? Yes, I did. Both my father and my grandfather, good men in many ways, had serious anger management problems. My dad had a short fuse and a loud voice, and he often scared me. He also embarrassed my mom and I with occasional fits of rage in public. When I related this to the counselor, he said, "You have the 'anger gene' and you grew up with anger in your atmosphere." He also assured me that if I was willing to work hard at it, I could control the problem.

Keep in mind that he said *control* the problem, not *cure* it. I spent several sessions with him, read some valuable resources he recommended, and committed myself to not ever hurting anyone again because I couldn't control my emotions or my tongue. I've kept that commitment.

My counselor also taught me some techniques that many people use successfully to manage their anger. Among them are taking several deep breaths, counting to ten slowly, and repeating calming words such as *peace, kindness,* or *love.* Another suggestion he made was to ask myself the following questions when I felt anger coming on: "What will the result be? Will my anger make things better or make things worse?"

Finally, he suggested that many people recite a calming quotation or verse from Scripture combined with prayer.

The counselor urged me to give all of them a try to see which one worked most effectively. I did, and found that each one works if done with that all-important commitment to not hurt anyone, including yourself. I eventually discovered that the verse from Scripture and prayer have the most calming effect on me, and I still use them to this day. Other people use different techniques that work better for them. The most important thing is to get help, whether professional or not, and to make the commitment.

Two bits of great news about emotional intelligence and self-control

1. They can be taught and they can be learned—We can't change our basic personality traits, the core physical characteristics we've inherited, or our native intelligence levels. They come to us naturally. But we *can* be taught and we *can* learn to raise our level of emotional intelligence and self-control. In fact, young people are learning these valuable social skills all over the country. Literally thousands of schools are now teaching social-emotional skills as part of their curriculum. Some operate under the banner of Character Education (more emphasis on ethical virtues), while others simply call it Social-Emotional Learning (more emphasis on social skills). When it's done effectively there are two results: school climate improves dramatically (it becomes a caring community) and academic performance improves.

2. Good social-emotional skills contribute to good character—Remember the title of the first chapter? "Good character is essential for a good life." That's why it's so important to learn how to control our emotions and to be in tune with the feelings of others. They're important parts of good character. Here's how the author concludes his great book, *Emotional Intelligence*:

> *There is an old-fashioned word for the body of skills that emotional intelligence represents:* **character**.
>
> —*Daniel Goleman, Ph.D.*

Personal Notes

PERSONAL NOTES

_____

_____

_____

_____

_____

_____

_____

_____

_____

_____

_____

_____

_____

_____

_____

_____

_____

_____

chapter 4 *Pain and suffering are part of life; so are healing and growth*

> *Bad things do happen; how I respond to them defines my character and the quality of my life. I can choose to sit in perpetual sadness, immobilized by the gravity of my loss, or I can choose to rise from the pain and treasure the most precious gift I have—life itself.*
>
> —*Walter Anderson*

Life is good, but sometimes it hurts

Way back in the introduction, I wrote that my goal was to write a short, practical, and upbeat book that would help people navigate life more effectively. While I *do* hope it has an upbeat and helpful message, I also want it to be realistic. It's not a "rah-rah" book claiming that you can or should be happy all the time. Life simply doesn't work that way. As much as I'd like to tell you that if you follow all the advice contained in these pages, nothing bad will ever happen to you, I can't. It would be a lie. The truth is that bad things happen to good people, often when they least deserve them.

For many years I taught psychology to teenagers in a high school and to working adults in a university. At the high school the course was called The Psychology of Personal Growth and Development. At the university I taught a series of courses in Organizational Behavior. Although the emphasis was on how individuals behave in groups (especially on the job), one course included a component on handling adversity and change. So, at both levels I taught a unit called "Pain and suffering; healing and growth." I introduced it by asking four simple questions:

1. "Is there pain and suffering in the world?"

Not surprising, 100 percent of the students at both levels answered yes.

2. "Have *you* ever felt pain and suffering?"

Again, everyone answered yes. A few of my adult students always felt the need to add, "Well, duh."

3. "Do you think you'll ever feel pain and suffering again?"

And for a third time, all the answers were yes. With a few more "Well, duh's."

4. "Do you always handle your pain and suffering in the most effective way possible?"

The answers weren't all yes to this question. Most of them were no, and with them came a variety of questions and comments, such as: "There isn't any good way to deal with pain. You just have to allow time to be the cure.", "Is there really a way that works?", "Are you going to teach us how to make pain and suffering go away?" To this last question, I answered, "No one can make it go away, but I do hope to teach you some things to do and not do when pain and suffering unexpectedly come upon us."

I said, "First, let's be specific. Based on your own experiences, what you've heard from others, and what you read, watch, and hear about in the news, please tell me some of the things that cause people pain." As they gave me their answers I wrote them on the chalkboard. Below is their list. The results were almost identical, no matter how many times I did this exercise.

Examples of pain and suffering

illness/disease	death of a child
loss of home	being paralyzed or handicapped
starvation	war and its effects
natural disasters	theft of something important
failure	being cheated
unemployment	being a victim of severe bullying
divorce	racial/sexual/age discrimination
death of parent	poverty in a country with no way out
child molesting	financial loss due to scam
victim of rape	terrorism and its effects
being an orphan	living in a country without freedom
being homeless	betrayal by someone you love and trust
drug/alcohol addiction	physical/verbal abuse by parent/spouse
end of a friendship	being wrongly accused of something
physical pain	death of friend or family member

In case you're wondering, the author has personally experienced fifteen, or half, of these "bad things" (some of them more than once), and knows people who have endured most of the others. Sadly, every one of them is going on in the world around us right at this moment. Chances are that at least a few of them have happened to you. And chances are that some of the others will happen to you at a time in the future.

The reality is that evil does exist. But I still believe, as did the famous musician, Luis Armstrong (1901-1971), that we live in "a wonderful world. " But it isn't a perfect world, so wise people throughout the ages have been teaching us both what *not* to do and what *to* do with the pain and suffering that are inevitable parts of life. We can not only heal, we can grow from painful experiences.

> *Every adversity, every failure, every heartache carries with it the seed of an equal or greater benefit.*
>
> —*Napoleon Hill*
>
> *Adversity brings wisdom.*
>
> —*Vietnamese proverb*

Six things to <u>not</u> do when hardship comes

Let me make an important point: everyone endures pain and suffering. It doesn't matter if you are young or old, educated or uneducated, rich or poor. It has nothing to do with your race, religion, physical appearance, or political beliefs. You will face hardship. The key is how you handle it. That's what this chapter is about. Here are six things people often do (the author has done all of them) when adversity comes, six things that will never improve a bad situation, six things that are virtually guaranteed to make matters worse:

1. Ask the question, "Why me?" This is the wrong question. The reality is that God, nature, or the cosmos didn't single you out for special punishment. Sometimes bad things happen to us because we deserve it, but they sometimes happen when we *don't* deserve it. This is what we have to learn to accept, as hard as it might be at times. When something good happens to you, do you ask, "Why me?" Probably not. When something bad and/or unfair happens to you there's a better question to ask yourself: "Now that this has happened, what's the best way to deal with it?"

2. Feel sorry for yourself. This usually follows closely behind "Why me?" That question really means, "This is unfair, and I don't deserve it." And it's followed by a full-blown "pity party." These sometimes last for days, even weeks. It will not only drag you down deeper, it's likely to drag your family and friends down with you. No one has fun at these kinds of parties. Instead of throwing a pity party, spend your time instead answering this question: "Now that this has happened, what's the best way to deal with it?"

3. Complain, whine, whimper, moan, and groan. This is nothing other than inviting as many people as possible to your "pity party." I promise you, no one wants to come. Do you like to hear other people whine? No. It ranks right up there with barking dogs, car alarms, crying babies, and the telephone busy signal as the most annoying sounds ever. Instead of whining, ask yourself this question: "Now that this has happened, what's the best way to deal with it?"

4. Let your anger get out of control (previously discussed in Chapter 3). Anger comes from frustration. It's a natural reaction when we face adversity that's outrageously unfair. But letting it get out of control is like pouring kerosene on a fire. You turn it into something bigger. You're likely to make the situation worse by hurting someone physically, hurting someone verbally, damaging property, getting hurt yourself, or getting into serious trouble. The key is to develop restraint, to control your emotions, to remind yourself to not make things worse. Put your energy instead into answering this question: "Now that this has happened, what's the best way to deal with it?"

5. Get even. Other people often cause some of our greatest pain. It's particularly upsetting when those other people are jarringly rude, mean-spirited, obnoxious, and uncaring. Our first reaction is to strike back, to get revenge. But when we do that we allow these other people to drag us down into the gutter with them. And it's also likely to make things worse rather than better. Once again, it takes restraint. It takes self-control. A better way to spend your time and energy is to ask yourself, "Now that this has happened, what's the best way to deal with it?"

> Seeking justice is one thing. But payback, revenge,
> and getting even aren't the same thing. They
> always make a bad situation worse. Take the high
> road instead.
>
> —Jane S. Guilford, Ph.D.

6. Cave in, give up, quit—Of the six things to *not* do when you face adversity, this is the worst one. Is there anything more pathetic than a quitter? Would you want others to think of you as a quitter? The world is full of inspiring stories about people who have come back from adversity. There isn't even one inspiring story about a person who quit. Quitters are wimps. People of strong character accept the challenge; they rise to the occasion. Instead of quitting, answer this question: "Now that this has happened, what's the best way to deal with it?"

> Never give up. Never, never, never, never give up.
>
> —Winston Churchill

Six things to <u>do</u> when hardship comes

There's almost universal agreement among behavioral scientists on what we *should* do when we go through hard times. Here are six of them. It's possible that doing just one of them will help a person deal effectively with the hurt he faces. It's also possible that a person facing adversity will employ a combination of them, or even all six. I mentioned earlier that I've tried all six of the things that *don't* work. I was younger then. And each one of them did, indeed, make matters worse.

As I got older, more experienced, and wiser, I learned to deal with adversity in more effective ways. It's valuable to know this because we never know when pain and suffering are coming. Sometimes they come when we least expect them and when we least deserve them. I've used all six of the suggestions listed and explained below. Let me assure you that they work. They don't make all the pain go away immediately, but they help us deal with it much more effectively.

1. Accept life as it is. Here's a good definition of wisdom: "a deep understanding and acceptance of how life works." This is what we're called to do when hardship comes: accept life as it is, not the way we want it to be or think it *should* be. This is the first, and most important, step in dealing with the challenges we face.

2. Talk about the problem. The worst thing you can do is keep the turmoil inside. Talk to someone you respect and trust. It might be a parent, grandparent, other relative, friend, mentor, pastor, teacher, coach, colleague, or professional counselor. It could be one or all of these. Share your pain and frustration; get it out so it can be examined and discussed. Then listen carefully to the insights and suggestions of these wise people.

3. Read or say an inspiring quotation or verse from Scripture. This is an amazingly simple, yet effective, way of reminding ourselves that people have been overcoming adversity for thousands of years. Many of them have left us with short and wise statements that help us deal with the problem rather than feel sorry for ourselves. So far in this chapter you've read five quotations about dealing with adversity.

These are good examples. There are three more at the end of the chapter.

4. Pray, and ask others to pray for you. This is not for everyone because not all people have faith. That's a statement of fact, not a judgment. I respect what people believe and don't believe. But prayer is a powerful tool in the life of one who has a sincere belief in God. It can provide courage, strength, confidence, and comfort. It also helps to have fellow believers pray for you and with you.

5. Read. When I was in my late 20s, and going through an excruciatingly painful experience, a dear friend gave me a book. It was *Man's Search For Meaning* by Viktor Frankl. This was the story of a man who faced indescribable adversity, loss, and suffering. But instead of feeling sorry for himself, he figured out ways to not only survive, but to triumph. This book was a great inspiration to me. It and many other books are available, and can do the same for you when facing hard times. Ask the people you turn to for comfort and advice to recommend a good book or two that will help you triumph as well.

6. Count your blessings; remind yourself about all the good things that happen. There's something we tend to forget when we're going through hard times. We forget that we have much to be thankful for and that far more good things happen than bad. The problem is that we take the good for granted. Count your blessings.

Here's a suggestion: write down the 20 things and the 20 people for which you're the most thankful. Keep the list in the Personal Notes section at the end of this chapter. The next time adversity comes, get the list out, read it slowly, and dwell on how thankful you should be for all the good people and things in your life. One of the things to be thankful for is that we don't have it as badly as do millions of others. And keep in mind that each time we're hurt, we have an opportunity to learn and to grow.

Words of wisdom for dealing with adversity

If I were asked to give what I consider the single most useful bit of advice for all humanity it would be this: Expect trouble as an inevitable part of life, and when it comes, hold your head high, look it squarely in the eye, and say, "I will be bigger than you. You cannot defeat me."

—Ann Landers

It takes courage to see in the reality around us and in us something ultimately positive and meaningful and live with it, even love it. Loving life is perhaps the highest form of the courage to be.

—Paul Tillich

Tough times never last, but tough people do.

—Robert Schuller

Personal Notes

PERSONAL NOTES

chapter
5 *Love is the cure that heals all wounds*

> *The cure for all ills and wrongs, the cares, the sorrows and the crimes of humanity, all lie in the one word 'love.' It is the divine vitality that everywhere produces and restores life.*
>
> —*Lydia Maria Child*

Four types of love

Since *love* is the first and most important word in this chapter, it's important that readers understand the definition the author is using. The dictionary I use contains eleven different definitions of love. They range from "feeling tender affection for someone" to "a score of zero in a tennis game." So, let's look at some of the different ways we refer to love. For instance, I love God and my faith, my wife Cathy, my family, my friends, other people, travel, reading, teaching, learning, sports, movies, food, technology, literature, cars, and physical fitness. I could go on, but you get the idea: the love of each of these is quite different.

Although any philosopher, psychologist, or religious leader could make a strong case that there are more or fewer than four types of love, I've chosen the following for the purpose of simplification. They're the types of love we're most aware of in our daily lives:

1. Love of God and one's faith
2. Love of others
3. Love of another person in a romantic way
4. Love of worldly things and activities

This chapter is mostly about the second type—love of others. But because all faiths teach us to love one another, it necessarily includes the first type as well—love of God. You don't have to believe in God to appreciate the wisdom of Biblical and philosophical teachings about loving one another. And you don't have to be a Buddhist or a Confucian to have great respect for their teachings. No one religion or philosophy has a monopoly on the world's wisdom, especially when it comes to love. There's remarkable consistency found in the writings about love by wise people of different belief systems throughout history. Following are some of them.

Great philosophers and religious leaders on love

- King Solomon (992-922 BC) taught that love makes amends for all our wrongs, that it brings healing to both the wrongdoer and the victim.

- Confucius (551-479 BC) said that love is wanting others to live fully, and helping them do so.

- Buddha (560-480 BC) wrote that love is wanting others to be happy, and that we become happier ourselves when we help them.

- Socrates (469-339 BC) stated that love lifts the weight and pain of life from both others and ourselves.

- Jesus (1 BC-33 AD—estimated) preached that we should love our neighbors (all people we meet) as we love ourselves, and that we should treat others as we would like them to treat us.

- Erich Fromm (1900-1980) a psychoanalyst and philosopher told us that we should be more concerned about *giving* love than *receiving* it.

- Morrie Schwatrz (1916-1995) in *Tuesdays With Morrie*, told writer Mitch Albom that the only way people find meaning in their lives is to devote themselves to loving other people.

- Billy Graham (1918-) said that if we love God we must love others, and that we will be known by our love.

- Pope Benedict XVI (1927-) teaches that the only way we can find true joy in life is to love others as God loves us.

You'll notice that there's a common thread to what all these wise people have written about love over the centuries: we find joy and meaning and love in our lives when we love others.

Two definitions of love

1. The best brief definition of loving others I could find is in the last sentence of the quotation by Lydia Maria Child used at the beginning of this chapter:

LOVE: *"IT IS THE DIVINE VITALITY THAT EVERYWHERE PRODUCES AND RESTORES LIFE."*

2. This is my own definition of loving others. It can be summed up in two words:

GIVING AND KINDNESS

I want to focus on GIVING here because KINDNESS is covered in Chapter 8. When you get there I hope you'll read it with the understanding that being loving and being kind are essentially the same.

What does it mean to be giving? What do we give that shows our love of others? Money? Empathy? Caring? Compassion? Listening? Service? All of these and more. Being giving means showing an unselfish concern for others, and acting on it. This often includes self-sacrifice. What do we give? We give ourselves to the betterment of others. We come to their aid, we teach them, we comfort them, we help them grow, we enhance their lives. The more we give to others, the more it comes back to us. We reap what we sow.

Think for a minute what the world would be like if everyone made their best effort at living each day with this type of love. Think for a minute what your individual world would be like if you made *your* best effort at living each day with this type of love. Does it seem impossible? To many it does, so they won't even try. But the truth is that there are literally millions of loving people throughout the world. Why don't we hear about them? Because the media prefers to publicize celebrities, criminals, perverts, the super wealthy, corrupt public officials, and cheaters. Loving people rarely make the news.

Yet these are the people who make the world a better place and make our lives better just from knowing them. They also teach us that when life is at its most painful, love is our only chance for genuine healing. As Lydia Maria Chid wrote, love "restores life."

Forgiveness is an important part of love

Please turn back to Chapter 4 and take another look at the examples of pain and suffering compiled by my students. After completing it, I asked them to divide it into two main types of pain. Most of them got it right away: physical and mental (also called social or emotional pain). Is one worse than the other? There wasn't complete agreement on this, but most felt it was emotional pain. Research supports this belief. Dr. Kip Williams, a psychologist from Purdue University, after completing four research projects with several colleagues, says that, "While both types of pain can hurt very much at the time they occur, social pain has the unique ability to come back over and over again, whereas physical pain lingers only as an awareness that it was indeed at one time painful."

Dr. Williams and his colleagues are not alone in that feeling. A few years ago I was watching a TV program about psychological healing that had several family therapists on it. One of them was Phil McGraw, the famous "Dr. Phil" who had his own nightly therapy show on TV. He was asked what the most difficult experience to recover from was. Without hesitating, he answered, "Betrayal. There's no greater pain, no greater anguish, than being betrayed by someone you love and trust." His colleagues on the program were all in agreement.

Also mentioned were romantic break-ups, cruelty, the end of a friendship, divorce, and being used by another person. In other words, the worst pain we'll ever feel is usually caused by people we were once very close to. As one of the therapists on the panel said, "The people we love and trust the most have the power to hurt us the most."

Every therapist on the panel also agreed that these kinds of hurtful experiences present the greatest challenge we'll ever face. The old expression that "Adversity makes us or breaks us" is true. Being hurt by someone we love and trust is the supreme test of the strength of our character. To be a loving person in these circumstances, to take the high road, and to be forgiving, is indeed a great challenge. But no matter how difficult it is, it's also the *only* way possible to bring about healing and the capacity to move on with life.

> *A loving heart is the beginning of all knowledge.*
>
> —*Thomas Carlyle*

A story of love and forgiveness

Many years ago, while I was experiencing the pain of being betrayed by someone I loved, I turned to Bill, one of my mentors who had gone through the same thing earlier in his life. He told me, "When trust in a loved one is violated it causes the most devastating pain in existence. First, you go through shock. You feel so violated. Then you just hurt. I felt like someone stuck a knife in me and ripped my entire insides out."

I asked him how he recovered from such a loss. His answer was, "It takes a long time. But we have to learn to deal with it, and we have to learn to move on. If we don't, we let it destroy us. I had the support of some great friends, talked to my pastor several times, read two powerful books, and saw a professional counselor for about three months. All of it was helpful."

He said the hardest part was learning to forgive. Both his pastor and his counselor told him it was the only way he'd be able to heal. His first reaction to both of them was, "No way! I'll never forgive her for what she did. But the more I was counseled, the more I read, and the more I thought about it, forgiveness made more and more sense. I learned that forgiveness is letting go of the pain, not letting it cripple you, and not giving the person who hurt you the power to continue to hurt you. It was sound advice spiritually, and it was sound advice psychologically. I felt like a huge load had been lifted from me when I finally learned how to forgive. Then I moved on with my life."

Bill added, "I hope you'll remember what I said about the power and freedom of forgiveness." Then he reached in his wallet and pulled out a small piece of paper that had been laminated with a thin plastic cover. On one side was the quotation by Lydia Maria Child at the beginning of this chapter. His counselor had given it to him, and he knew he needed to look at it often, so he carried it with him everywhere he went. On the other side was a verse from Scripture that his pastor had given him. It said, "For if you forgive other people their failures, your Heavenly Father will also forgive you"—Matthew 6:14.

Learning to forgive was even harder than I thought it would be. I remembered Bill saying, "First, you go through shock. You feel so violated. Then you just hurt." I did, indeed, hurt for a long time. And there were times, like my mentor, when I thought learning to forgive was impossible. It was, without question, the hardest life lesson I ever learned. But it was also one of the most valuable. It helped me put the pain behind and get on with my life.

> *The practice of forgiveness is our most important contribution to the healing of the world.*
>
> —Marianne Williamson

What it means to be loving and kind

It means being humble, developing empathy, showing compassion, having patience, giving of yourself, and forgiving those who have hurt you.

> *Eventually you will come to understand that*
> *love heals everything, and love is all there is.*
>
> —*Gary Zukav*

Personal Notes

Personal Notes

part 2 *Seven Choices that Determine the Quality of Life*

We must make the choices that enable us to fulfill the deepest capacities of our real selves.

—*Thomas Merton*

There's a commonly shared belief that the average person has at least five "defining moments" in his or her lifetime. Sometimes they're called "aha" or "I get it" moments. Something happens that causes us to see life in a different way, and we change because of it. We have a new perspective on life, a new understanding.

One of my defining moments occurred when I was 17. It was at a freshman orientation meeting at the University of San Francisco. The president of the university said, "You're not here so we can *fill* your minds. You're here so we can *open* your minds." That got my attention, but he said something a few minutes later that has affected my thinking every day since then. He said, "The greatest gift God gave you is a free will. He didn't create you as a puppet, but as a person with the power and freedom to make choices. During your four years here we're going to try to help you learn to make choices that enrich not only your own life, but the lives of others."

He reminded us that we make hundreds of choices every day. "Those choices," he said, "eventually determine the quality of your lives." Seven of those choices are discussed in this section.

chapter *Attitude is the most impor-*
6 *tant factor in determining*
success or failure

> *Our attitudes propel us forward toward our victories
> or bog us down in defeat. They are the foothold
> beneath us in every step we take. Our attitudes
> make us rich or poor, happy or unhappy, fulfilled or
> incomplete. They are the single most determining
> factor in every action we will ever make. We and
> our attitudes are inextricably combined; we are our
> attitudes and our attitudes are us.*
>
> —Shad Helmstetter, Ph.D.

Defining a key word

As *love* was the first and most important word in the previous chapter, *attitude* is the first and most important word in this chapter. And again, it's valuable for readers to know how the author is defining it. While there are many kinds of love, there are only two kinds of attitudes: good and bad. Here's the definition we'll use:

ATTITUDE IS EVERY PERSON'S "CONTROL CENTER." IT'S A FRAME OF MIND—THE WAY WE VIEW AND APPROACH EVERY ASPECT OF LIFE. IT'S ALSO AN EXPECTATION. IF WE HAVE A POSITIVE ATTITUDE WE EXPECT THE BEST, AND ACT ACCORDINGLY. IF WE HAVE A NEGATIVE ATTITUDE WE EXPECT THE WORST, AND ACT ACCORDINGLY. WE REAP WHAT WE SOW.

To be more specific, here are some basic differences between people with good and bad attitudes:

PEOPLE WITH A GOOD ATTITUDE	PEOPLE WITH A BAD ATTITUDE
Are optimistic —look for the good	Are pessimistic —look for the bad
See possibilities and opportunities	See problems and obstacles
Are thankful for the good in life	Complain about the bad in life
Motivate themselves	Wait to be motivated
Accept hardship and deal with it	Feel sorry for themselves
Are determined and work hard	Are unfocused and give up easily
Upbeat—lift the spirits of others	Downbeat—drag others down

The benefits of having a positive attitude—

Researchers at the Mayo Clinic, one of the most highly regarded medical facilities in the world, have concluded that optimistic people live longer and healthier, endure less stress, enjoy life more, deal more effectively with hardship, are more adventurous, have more friends, and are more successful in their careers.

The best thing about a good attitude? It's *always* a choice. Anyone can have one.

What determines your attitude at any given moment?

Above is a question that I used to write on the chalkboard in my classroom. I gave all the students a half sheet of paper, and asked them to answer the question briefly in writing. I asked them to not say anything out loud until everyone had written their answer. I wanted all the students to get their thoughts on paper without being influenced by the students who spoke up first. Here are the answers I received most frequently:

> "It depends on the mood I'm in."

> "The day of the week—bad mood on Monday, good mood on Friday."

> "Where I am."

> "What I'm doing."

> "It all depends on whom I'm with."

> "Which class I'm in."

> "The weather."

> Occasionally, I would have a student write, "It doesn't matter. I *always* have a good attitude." I loved it!

You'll notice that almost all of the students said their attitudes were determined by the circumstances they were in. I said, "According to your answers, your attitudes are always determined by something outside yourself. You have no choice in the matter, and no control over them. Your attitudes are held captive by people, places, times, things, and conditions." They looked a little puzzled. This was good because it meant they were thinking, something teachers love to get their students to do.

I said with a big smile, and in a lame attempt to be dramatic: "WRONG, WRONG, WRONG! I am now about to teach you the most valuable thing you'll ever learn from me. Here it is: **Your attitude is the most important choice you'll ever make.** You make this choice every minute of every day, and it will influence literally everything you do. Look upon your attitude as the engine that runs your life. The most important thing to understand about this is that your attitude will ALWAYS be a choice, no matter what your circumstances are." I saw more puzzled looks. And not surprisingly, several students said they had never heard this before. I assured them I hadn't heard of it when I was their age either. And I promised them, "If you grasp this—and apply it—it will be one of the most valuable things you'll ever learn, and it will provide you with the most powerful tool you'll ever have."

There were some legitimate questions about how one could choose a good attitude during times of great loss. I reminded them about a previous lesson about pain and suffering, healing and growth (Chapter 4). I also resorted to one of the most powerful tools a teacher has: storytelling.

Two true stories about choosing an attitude

1. Bruce Diaso

When I was a 19-year-old sophomore at the University of San Francisco, I met an 18-year-old freshman who had a profound effect on my life. Why? Because he had the greatest attitude of anyone I've ever known. I met Bruce early in the school year, but didn't get to really know him until the spring semester, when he taught me one of the most valuable lessons I've ever learned.

Bruce had been a great high school football player in his hometown of Fresno, California, and was planning to attend Notre Dame University on an athletic scholarship. But tragedy hit him at the beginning of his senior year. He was stricken with polio a few weeks before the Salk Polio Vaccine arrived at his school. He almost died, was in the hospital for several weeks, and ended up paralyzed. He could not move his legs or his arms. He could talk, he could move his head, and he could move his hands and fingers, even though his arms were dead.

Through sheer determination and hard work, he earned an academic scholarship to USF. His caretakers were his roommate and a few other guys who lived in dorm rooms nearby. Without being able to move his arms or legs, you can imagine how much they had to do for him. I always admired them because they cared for Bruce so unselfishly and so lovingly.

Bruce was, without question, the most admired and loved student at the university in the four years he was there. Why, because people felt sorry for him? Absolutely not. It was because he was always a delight to be around. He had a big smile and a good word for everyone. He was also brilliant and an unbelievably dedicated student. He wanted to learn everything.

One day I had occasion to eat lunch with Bruce. It was rare because he usually had a crowd of people around him. But we both went for an early lunch that day and found ourselves in an almost empty dining commons. I had always wondered about his amazing attitude, and decided that this would be a good time to learn more about it. I knew almost nothing about psychology at the time, so I asked Bruce if he had been born with his incredible attitude. He laughed, and said, "No, Hal, I promise you I wasn't born with this attitude. I learned to develop it. I learned that it's a *choice*, and that anyone can have the same attitude I have."

Because I wanted to have an attitude like his, I said, "Bruce, please tell me your secret." He laughed again, and said there was no secret. He said when he got polio and learned that he would never walk or lift his arms again, he sunk into a deeply negative funk. He said the two words that best described his attitude were: **anger** and **self-pity.** His doctor challenged him one day by asking if the anger and self-pity were making things better or making things worse. He said, "Bruce, change your attitude, change your life." Bruce realized immediately what the doctor was trying to tell him: he was poisoning himself. And he realized it was his *choice* to do so.

Bruce thought it about it for a few days, and eventually chose two new words that would define his attitude: **thankfulness** and **opportunity.** He said he was thankful for all the things he used to take for granted. Among them were God (he believed there was reason for everything), his parents, siblings, friends, teachers, his country, intelligence, his education, and all the opportunities he saw in life despite his handicap. I suddenly realized that I had all the same things in my life (without the handicap), and had always taken them for granted.

My conversation with Bruce that day turned out to be what I referred to earlier as a "defining moment." It changed my attitude, and it changed my life. The most important thing Bruce taught me was that attitude—he called it the "control center" of our lives—was a **choice.** He said, "Whether you're in perfect health or have a handicap like mine, you can choose your attitude any minute of the day." He finished his lesson with a question that I've never forgotten: "Do you realize that being able to choose your own attitude is the greatest power and the greatest freedom that you'll ever have?"

Bruce graduated from the University of San Francisco *summa cum laude* (Latin for "with highest honor"). He accepted a scholarship to the law school, where his success story continued. Three years later he again graduated with the highest honors. He turned down several high-paying salaries from prestigious law firms all over the country. Instead, he accepted a position as a Public Defender in his home town of Fresno. He devoted the rest of his life to helping people who were poor and in trouble. He also did free legal work for charitable organizations, and was given awards for his public service while he was still in his 20s.

Sadly, Bruce died when he was only 31. His paralyzed and weak body eventually gave out. A dear friend of mine who was one of Bruce's caretakers for six years told me shortly after the funeral that he learned more about life from Bruce than anyone he'd ever known. He also told me something that I still find astounding more than 40 years later. He said in the six years he lived with Bruce he saw him in great pain and in poor health, but he kept on and always gave his best. And never once did he hear Bruce complain about anything.

I told Bruce's story to my students every year since he died in 1972. It made an impact on most of them, and it was a valuable lesson about the power and freedom we have to choose our attitudes no matter what the circumstances. I also gave them an assignment. It was called "The Bruce Diaso Memorial Challenge." I challenged them to go one day (24 hours) without complaining about anything. They tried, but failed. It literally took me 23 years before I found a student who could do it. Her name is Grace. She said, "I just thought of something I should be thankful for every time I started to complain. You know, Dr. Urban, we have a lot more to be thankful for than we do to complain about." It would have made Bruce happy. He touched many people during his short life, and he's still touching them today. If you want to have a good life, start here: remind yourself that your attitude is your "control center," and that it's always a choice.

2. Viktor Frankl

Frankl and his magnificent book, *Man's Search for Meaning*, were mentioned briefly in Chapter 4. Here is his story in more detail: Frankl was a brilliant young Jewish psychotherapist in

Austria in the earlier 1940s. This was during World War II, when a madman named Adolph Hitler decided that he and his fellow Nazis would kill every Jew in the world after first herding them into concentration camps and subjecting them to unspeakable degradation and torture. Called the Holocaust, it resulted in the genocide of more than six million Jews and an additional five million other innocent people considered inferior due to race, religion, and disability.

Dr. Frankl had his wife, mother, father, and brother taken from him. They were sent to a different concentration camp than he was, and all were executed. He also had his home, his medical practice, and all his earthly possessions taken from him. The Nazis shaved his head, branded a number onto his arm, and subjected him and his fellow inmates to horrendous living conditions and inflicted indescribable torture upon them.

Some of Frankl's friends were beaten to death, some simply gave up and died, and others committed suicide, believing there was no hope. Frankl decided that he was not only going to survive, but go on to make a contribution to mankind. He asked himself a question: what is something the Nazis can never take away from me? He decided that he had one freedom left, and that no one could take it from him unless he allowed it.

> *Everything can be taken from a man but one thing: the last of human freedoms—to choose one's attitude in any given set of circumstances, to choose one's own way.*
>
> *—Viktor Frankl*

This is a simple, yet profound, concept. And it can be as life-changing for any of us as it was for Frankl. We don't have control over everything that happens to us, but we do have control over how we'll deal with what happens. This powerful thought has helped millions of people overcome adversity instead of giving up. Frankl was freed by Allied forces in 1945, and went on to become one of the most influential psycho-therapists of all time. He taught us that the ability to choose our own attitude, no matter what the circumstances are, is the greatest freedom and the greatest power we'll ever have.

What determines *your* attitude at any given moment?

> *The greatest discovery of my generation is that human beings can alter their lives by altering their attitudes.*
>
> —*William James*

Personal Notes

PERSONAL NOTES

chapter 7 *Honesty builds trust and strong relationships; dishonesty destroys them*

*Honesty is the best policy. If I lose mine honor,
I lose myself.*

—William Shakespeare

Being authentic

I wish I could tell you that I understood at a young age how important honesty was and that I've been consistently truthful throughout my life. But that wouldn't be honest. I mentioned earlier that I went through a bad spell in my young adulthood. It included some dishonesty (nothing major or criminal), and I get a feeling of shame every time I think about it. Shortly after getting back on track I came to the conclusion that of all the virtues, honesty is among the most important.

Why? Because it's the one that makes you an authentic person, a person of integrity. It's the one that cements the other virtues together. This is probably the reason why one of the greatest leaders in the history of our country wrote more than 200 years ago that:

Honesty is the first chapter in the book of wisdom.

—*Thomas Jefferson*

You can do all the other things I suggest in this book, but if being honest isn't one of them, you'll never know or experience the true meaning of success, and you'll never know the real meaning of integrity. Integrity, often used interchangeably with honesty, is actually a broader term. In regard to human nature, it means being complete. It comes from the word *integral,* which means "whole or undivided." Merriam-Webster defines it as "essential to completeness."

An online dictionary I use occasionally defines integrity this way:

1. Adherence to moral and ethical principles
2. Soundness of moral character; honesty
3. The state of being whole, entire, or uncompromised

Integrity is number one on my list of most important virtues. Though no one is perfect, there's no way around integrity if you want to lead and succeed in life. Integrity is similar to honesty, but it goes deeper by directly relating to values, morals, and character.

—*Jackie Christiansen*
Executive success coach

Complete people are honest in all aspects of life and consistently live by high ethical and moral standards. They earn self-respect as well as the respect of others. They build trust and develop a solid reputation with family and friends, and later with business associates. To live without integrity is to be both deceitful and phony. People who are dishonest cheat themselves out of that wonderful contentment we call inner peace, and they prevent themselves from fully developing, from being all they can be. Dishonesty retards both our personal and social development, and keeps us from knowing the beauty of a clear conscience.

Albert Schweitzer (1875-1965), a Nobel Peace Prize winner and one of the greatest persons who ever lived, often used the phrase "reverence for life." He said we can't have it unless we develop a personal code of ethics which includes truthfulness in all our dealings with other people. He wrote that only after we develop this type of integrity can we "feel at home in this world," and be truly effective in it. Honesty, in Schweitzer's view, is the most basic element in the character of people who have a genuine respect for life.

Advice from the wisest Americans

My belief that honesty is one of our most important choices and one of the most important virtues has been strongly reinforced by Dr. Karl Pillemer, a Cornell University professor who has done extensive research on people over the age of 65. He calls them "the wisest Americans." His 2011 book, *30 Lessons for Living,* is the result of interviewing more than a thousand seniors over a five-year period. He doesn't claim that old age automatically makes a person wise, but those he interviewed about their most valuable life lessons were, indeed, among the wisest people he had ever met. Basically, he asked them what advice they'd like to pass on to the next generation. In other words, you and your friends and colleagues.

In a section of the book called, "The First Lesson: Always Be Honest," Dr. Pillemer says the elders he interviewed were unanimous in their opinion that honesty is the primary prescription for regret-free living. When asked what the major values and principles they lived by were, virtually all of them had honesty or integrity in their responses. He also comments on some of the other great virtues these people had developed.

But he concludes by saying, "Yet from the enormous list of possible virtues to recommend, one in particular was mentioned over and over: **always be honest**. It's up to you, but if you choose to ignore it, don't say they didn't warn you!"

> *If I could only give three words of advice to my children, they would be, "Tell the truth." If I got three more words, I'd add, "All the time."*
>
> *—Randy Pausch*

"Is honesty still the best policy?"

The question above was at the top of a survey I gave to my students every year. Please answer the questions the same way they did—by circling the Yes or the No at the end of each.

1. If you bought any product, from a home to a cell phone, would you want the salesperson to be honest with you about it? Yes No

2. If you owned a business, would you want your employees to be honest in dealing with customers and in submitting expense accounts? Yes No

3. If you were riding in a cab, would you want the driver to take the most direct and least expensive route to your destination? Yes No

4. If you lost your wallet, along with cash, driver's license, and credit cards, would you want the person who found it to return it to you fully intact? Yes No

5. If you invested some of your hard-earned money, would you want the financial adviser to be completely honest with you about both the risks and the rewards? Yes No

6. If you were married or in a serious relationship, would you want your loved one to always be honest with you? Yes No

7. If you were competing in an athletic event, would you want the officials and your opponents to conduct themselves honorably? Yes No

8. If you're an employee or a student, do you want your work and achievements to be evaluated fairly, honestly, and on their merits? Yes No

9. If you bought a product with a credit card over the phone or on the Internet, would you want the person handling the transaction to honor your privacy and security? Yes No

10. If you were a recording artist or studio owner, would you want people to buy your music in a legal and honest manner? Yes No

I conducted this survey with my students, including my adult students at the university, literally hundreds of times. It probably won't surprise you that on every question, 100 percent of the answers were Yes. One of my high school students made a telling remark one day as we were discussing their answers. He said, "This is different. No one wants to be ripped off. No one wants to be cheated. These questions are all about how we want other people to be honest us." I looked at him, then at the rest of the class, smiled, and said, "Exactly!" He thought for a moment, and then said, "Oh, now I see what you're getting at. You're saying that if we don't like it when people aren't honest with us, then we should be honest with others." I thanked him for helping me make my point. As always, a very meaningful discussion about honesty and dishonesty followed. I don't claim that I turned every student into a person of total integrity that day, but some good seeds were planted.

The two most common excuses for being dishonest

I always found the unit on honesty and integrity to be one of the most challenging to teach, especially to teenagers. The reason was that I had to overcome two strong mindsets. Many of my students were already jaded, cynical, and mistrusting. Some of them even said they had learned from their parents why you sometimes have to be dishonest. I knew what was coming, but I still asked, "Why?" Here are the two reasons I heard every year:

1. "Everyone does it." We live in a very competitive society, and most other people are cheating or lying, or both. If we don't do it also we won't be able to keep up. Among the examples given were school, business, politics, sports, and filing income taxes.

2. "It's only wrong if you get caught." Only the stupid people get caught. Lying and cheating here and there are part of the game, and the smart people learn to play it well.

My response to both? "Those are myths—very dangerous myths. They've been repeated so many times, people start to believe them. That's what a myth is—a falsehood that's been passed around for a long time. I'll admit that there's way too much dishonesty in the world, but not *everyone* is lying and cheating. Honest people don't get a lot of publicity, but there are millions of them. And whether you get caught or not, dishonesty is *always* wrong. Your Yes answers on the survey are proof that you don't want anyone to cheat you or lie to you. Therefore, it's wrong, whether you get caught or not."

Reaping what we sow applied to honesty and dishonesty

My students always told me that the part of the unit on honesty that had the biggest impact on them was when the class worked together on compiling a list of consequences of both dishonest and honest behavior. I've written about them in two of my previous books. So you don't have to go look them up elsewhere (or buy another book), here they are:

The price we pay for being dishonest:

1. We ruin our relationships—all strong relationships are based on trust.

2. We damage our reputations—no one likes or trusts a dishonest person.

3. We form bad habits—if we "get away" with doing something dishonest, we're more likely to do it again and again and again.

4. We eventually get caught and get into trouble—dishonesty always catches up to us. Sometimes the punishment is severe.

5. We hurt innocent people—being betrayed by someone we trust is one of life's most painful experiences.

6. We can end our careers—millions of people throughout history have lost their jobs (along with their reputations) because of dishonesty.

7. We damage our health—it's been proven that we attack our own nervous systems with each deceitful act. The result is stress and strain.

8. We become phonies and manipulators—dishonesty can become a way of life. We begin to lose sight of the truth, and we use other people.

9. We punish ourselves—all acts of dishonesty prevent us from being authentic, from being a complete person, and from knowing inner peace.

10. We have to live with regret—no one can undo a dishonest act. You can admit it, apologize, and be forgiven, but you'll always have to live with it.

The rewards of being honest:

1. We have peace of mind—this is the best reward of all. It's always comforting to know that we did the right thing, that we told the truth.

2. We build and maintain strong relationships—trust is the bond that holds them together.

3. We develop good character—once we experience the feelings of self-worth that come from being honest, we work even harder at being honorable.

4. We earn a good reputation—honesty always wins; it shines through. And people respect us for it.

5. We contribute to our health—we free ourselves from guilt, worry, stress, and instead enjoy feelings of self-respect and confidence.

6. We are authentic—when we're honest, we develop a strong sense of what it means to be real rather than phony.

7. We have fewer regrets and less guilt—the less we do wrong, the less we have to fret about it.

8. We stay out of trouble—the more honest we are, the more freedom we have.

9. We gain self-respect—we like and respect honest people, including ourselves.

10. We become complete—honesty and integrity make us fully human.

Honesty is rewarding, but always a challenge

Being honest is hard work. In fact, all the virtues are hard work—yet always worth the effort.

—Erwin G. Hall

A mentor I had many years ago was among the most honest persons I've ever known. He told me that being honest is one of the greatest challenges he faces. I was surprised. I figured once you see the rewards and get into the habit of being honest, it would become easier. He assured me that that's not always the case. We live in a dishonest world and in a society that sometimes even glorifies dishonesty. Because we're surrounded by it, the temptation to take moral shortcuts (as so many others are doing) is often great. I asked him how he managed to maintain his integrity. He answered, " I remind myself that 'we reap what we sow.' I like peace of mind."

Honesty is its own reward. Nothing beats a clear conscience.

—Nicholas Prati

Personal Notes

Personal Notes

chapter 8 *Every act of kindness makes the world a better place, and you a better person*

> *You may be sorry that you spoke, sorry you stayed or went, sorry you won or lost, sorry so much was spent. But as you go through life, you'll never be sorry you were kind.*
>
> —Herbert V. Prochnow

Respect is important — kindness is even more important

The title of Chapter 8 in *Life's Greatest Lesson* is "Good people build their lives on a foundation of respect." Respect, which has deteriorated enormously in our society in recent years, is just as important as it was in 1990 when I wrote that first book—maybe even more important. It is, indeed, the foundation of all civil societies and relationships among the people in them. I see respect as having these four pillars:

1. Manners—Being polite, being considerate of others, being courteous, treating other people with respect and dignity.

2. Language—Using positive and clean words that nourish the atmosphere rather than negative and dirty words that poison it. Using kind words to build people up rather than mean words to tear them down.

3. Honoring the rules—Rules have often been called "guidelines for good human relations." The great philosopher Aristotle said that when we honor the rules we act in such a way that benefits the community as a whole.

4. Appreciating and respecting all persons—People are different in many ways. We must respect the dignity, rights, and worth of all persons regardless of differences in race, religion, mental ability, sexual orientation, or social class.

You'll note that this book has a chapter about kindness, not about respect. There's a good reason. As important as respect is, kindness is even more important. It's more important for the simple reason that it includes several other virtues, including respect. You can be respectful without being kind, but you can't be kind without being respectful. Let me explain by using one of my favorite and most frequently used books, *Merriam-Webster's Collegiate Dictionary*. Here are some of the ways the word *kind* is defined in it: "affectionate, loving, sympathetic and helpful nature, gentle, giving pleasure and/or relief to others, gracious, considerate, courteous." So, not only is kindness more inclusive than respect, it's also more challenging. It's hard work to be consistently kind. But the rewards are great. The kindness we practice has a way of coming back to us. We reap what we sow.

It is one of the most beautiful compensations
of this life that no man can sincerely try to help
another without helping himself.

—*Ralph Waldo Emerson*

Defining kindness

> *Kindness is being humble enough to know that other people count just as much as you do. Kindness is being compassionate. Kindness is a lifestyle that always involves helping others.*
>
> —Marilyn Ecklund

Because kindness is so important and has so many aspects, it needs a definition just for this chapter so you'll know specifically how the author is using the term. In my opinion, kindness has six major components, all of which are defined below. I'm defining them in terms of what kind people consistently *do*. They put these virtues into action.

1. Kind people are humble. The nicest, most caring, most loved, and most admired people I know are all humble. Instead of a "me first" attitude, they have an "others first" attitude. They don't brag, they don't try to be the center of attention, and they don't always need to have their own way. Instead, they look out for others, always being considerate of their needs and feelings. It's no wonder that the ancient and wise philosopher Confucius said that becoming humble is the starting place for developing the other virtues.

The best way to define humility is to share with you one of my favorite and most meaningful quotations. It had a big impact on me at a time when I was trying to overcome a serious case of self-centeredness. Nothing helped me more than these words, which I still read every morning:

> *This is the greatest and most useful lesson we can learn: to know ourselves for what we truly are, to admit freely our weaknesses and failings, and to hold a humble opinion of ourselves because of them. Not to dwell on ourselves and always to think well and highly of others is great wisdom.*
>
> —Thomas A' Kempis

2. Kind people develop empathy. Empathy is the ability to understand and be sensitive to what another person is feeling. It doesn't come naturally because we have a tendency to think about our own feelings first. Empathy is the opposite. It's putting the other person's feelings first. Kind people develop empathy by asking themselves, "How would I feel if this had just happened to me?" From this comes the ability to put ourselves into another person's position and feel what he or she is feeling. These feelings can be great joy or deep sadness, or anything in between. Psychologists tells us that empathy is the starting block for all forms of kindness, especially compassion.

> It's been proven that those who read and deal effectively with other people's feelings are at an advantage in any domain of life. Empathy is the fundamental 'people skill.'
>
> —Daniel Goleman, Ph.D.

3. Kind people show compassion. Compassion is the next step after developing empathy. It means taking *action* to help those who are in need. Obviously, we can't help all the people in the world who are suffering, but we can help family members, friends, and people in our communities. Sometimes it means simply spending time with someone just to listen and to be comforting. Sometimes it means giving money to an organization that helps the needy. And sometimes it means pitching in to help either an individual or a group in order to improve a bad situation.

Here's one of the best examples of compassion I could possibly give you:

My mom, Ruth Urban, the kindest and most caring person I've ever known, came to live with my wife Cathy and me during the last year of her life. She was dying of leukemia.

As much as we loved taking care of her, you can probably imagine that it was time-consuming and emotionally draining. One of the hardest parts was that we could never leave the house together. One of us had to be here all the time. We couldn't go out to dinner, we couldn't go to a movie or to a ball game, and we couldn't go away for the weekend.

Fortunately for us, two of our dearest friends, John and Susanne, have both empathy and compassion, and they came to the rescue without even being asked. They knew what we were going through, and even though they live three and a half hours away, they drove to our home two times during that year so Cathy and I could get away for a few days. They gave my mom the same loving care that we gave her, while Cathy and I were able to rest, relax, enjoy each other, and recharge our batteries. John and Susanne made great personal sacrifices twice to help us in a time of need, and their loving acts will be appreciated and remembered for the rest of our lives. This is compassion.

> *If you want others to be happy, practice compassion.*
> *If you want to be happy, practice compassion.*
>
> —*Dalai Lama*

4. Kind people are patient. The best definition I could find of patience was provided by a wonderful organization known as The Virtues Project: "Patience is being calm and tolerant when difficult things happen." In this author's opinion, there are two types of "difficult things": 1. Occurrences—some examples are being stopped in traffic, waiting in a long line at the Post Office or a store, or simply having something go wrong, especially when we're in a hurry. 2. People—as you already know, some people are very difficult to deal with. There could be a wide variety of reasons why they're that way. Kind people remain calm and tolerant. They don't get in the difficult person's face and make matters worse.

This doesn't mean that you have to stand idly by while someone is being intolerably rude or mean. It means that you should do your best to handle the situation in a way that cools things down rather than adds kerosene to the fire. I'm speaking from experience as one who in the past made a lot of fires bigger. In fact, I even created quite a few due to lack of patience. I was a full-blown "hot head"—quick-tempered, impatient, confrontational, and loud.

And what did my impatience (lack of self-control) accomplish? I made matters worse, scared people, hurt other people's feelings, and hurt myself. It took two wise mentors (patient ones) a long time to convince me that I could learn to be patient. And I finally got it. Even today, I still fight the tendency to be impatient, but I remind myself to not make things worse. The greatest reward of patience? A more peaceful life. We reap what we sow.

How can we expect to have others accept our weaknesses unless we are willing to accept theirs? Patience, then, is about respect for others.

—Chuck Gallozzi

5. Kind people are giving. What do they give? They give themselves. There's an old saying that claims "it's better to give than it is to receive." Kind people not only understand this, they put it into practice. They're generous with their time and their resources and they love to help people in whatever way they can. Winston Churchill said that we make a living by what we *get*, but we make a life by what we *give*. In other words, we enrich our own lives while we enrich the lives of others. We reap what we sow.

Success in life has nothing to do with what you gain or accomplish for yourself. It's what you do for others.

—Danny Thomas (1912-1991) Actor and founder of St. Jude's Hospital for children with cancer

6. Kind people are forgiving. Let me warn you: forgiveness is one of the most difficult virtues to develop. Here's something I wrote about it in a previous book: "Learn to forgive. It's incredibly hard, but worth the effort—and essential to mental health." Like patience, forgiveness can be learned. I had a lot of help from a mentor on this one also. When I finally got it, I felt a new sense of freedom and renewal.

As I wrote in Chapter 5, forgiveness doesn't mean that you have to accept the wrongdoing of another person. It means that you're letting go of it and moving on with your life. Forgiveness is letting go of the past, and enjoying the present instead. Forgiveness is a form of healing which allows us to put the hurt behind us. It's what a kind and loving person does.

Keep in mind that forgiveness is a sign of strength. Some people almost proudly claim that they'll "never forgive," as if it's something to be admired. It isn't—it's a sign of weakness. Real forgiveness requires character, particularly courage.

> *Life may not be perfect, but you can learn to suffer less.*
> *You can learn to forgive, and you can learn to heal.*
> —*Dr. Fred Luskin, author of* **Forgive For Good**

If the author could do it all over again

A few weeks after the publication of *Choices That Change Lives,* I was interviewed on a Minneapolis TV station by a woman who was absolutely convinced that I not only had it all figured out, but also led a perfect life. She came to these conclusions based on what she had read from two of my books.

I did everything I could to convince her that I, like everyone else, was still a work in progress. I was getting better, but still had a long way to go.

I also did everything I could to convince her that I don't even come close to leading a perfect life. I told her that I had several flaws. Some of them I've been able to correct through the learn-from-your-mistakes method. But some of the others seem to want to hang around. They remind me that I have a lot more work to do. That's a big part of life—working on our flaws. I also mentioned to her that I wish I could do some parts of my life over, the ones that haunt me the most.

This comment set up her next question. She asked, "If you *could* do it all over again, what would you do differently?" I answered without hesitation, "I would be a lot kinder." She seemed genuinely surprised, and said, "But you write about all these virtues, and you seem so nice." I told her that writing about virtues and being nice on TV while promoting a book are one thing; consistently putting those virtues into practice—especially kindness—is another thing. I added, "I have some great regrets about the many times that I *wasn't* kind. And as I said earlier, these slip-ups can haunt us for a lifetime." I reminded her about something she had interviewed me about a few years earlier. I had written in my second book, *Positive Words, Powerful Results*, that two of the most powerful and healing phrases we can ever say are:

"I was wrong"
"I'm sorry"

What does it mean to be kind? It means being humble, developing empathy, showing compassion, having patience, giving of yourself, and forgiving those who have hurt you.

> *Kindness is its own reward. It has a way of returning to us. We reap what we sow.*
>
> —*Nita Severns, Ph.D., Psychologist*

Personal Notes

Personal Notes

chapter 9 *Achievement is the result of hard work; do the best you can with what you have*

No one ever achieved anything important the "quick and easy way." That's because a substitute for hard work still hasn't been discovered—and never will be.

—Grace J. Harris

Life is hard work

Back in the early 1980s, some of my high school freshmen were complaining, out loud and in a whiny tone, about how hard it was to complete what I considered to be a simple in-class geography assignment. For the most part, American students at all grade levels are geographically illiterate. So, they become uncomfortable when their lack of knowledge is exposed. I gave each student an atlas, a blank map, and a list of countries, cities, and bodies of water. All they were required to do was find those places in the atlas and put them on their blank maps. Some of the kids went right to work on it, but too many of them were whining that, "This is hard," and asking, "Why do you make us work so much?"

This whining and grumbling about being required to actually work in school led to one of the most meaningful class discussions I'd ever had. In my first few years as a teacher I was told by a mentor to always look for what we call "teachable moments," especially if they had something to do with life lessons. So here were my responses to their two comments above:

Student: "This is hard work." (with frown and whiny tone)

My response: "Good, because *life* is hard work." (with a smile and up- beat tone)

Student: "Why do you make us work so much?" (with frown and whiny tone)

My response: "Because that's my job—to help you learn. That's what learning is: hard work. In this case, it's learning where some important places are in the world. And that's what life is: hard work. You can't separate the two because if you want to have a good life, learning should never stop. Learning in school is just the beginning." (with a smile and up-beat tone)

Somehow, this concept of life being hard and learning being hard got their attention. So we strayed from the geography assignment for a few minutes, and I switched from teaching an academic lesson to teaching a life lesson. I wrote the following on the chalkboard:

Life is hard work.
Life should be ...

Then I asked them to complete the second sentence. Almost all of them responded, "... easy and fun." I went back to the chalkboard and wrote:

Learning is hard work.
Learning should be ...

I wasn't surprised, and you're probably not surprised, that I received the same response: "easy and fun."

Early in my teaching career I discovered than a high percentage of my students hadn't even begun to learn how life really works. So many of them came to high school spoiled, with an unrealistic notion that *work* was a dirty word, and that the primary function of a teacher was to entertain them. It didn't take long for me to become passionate about helping them understand some of the realities of life.

I grew up in the 1940s and 1950s (yes, I'm that old) with a clear message from my parents, from my teachers, from my employers, and from society: **If you want to be successful in life, you'll have to work for it. You'll have to give up some things along the way, but in the long run, your hard work and sacrifice will pay off.** It was a simple, straightforward message, and I never questioned it. It served me and millions of my generation well.

Things have changed dramatically since I was growing up, and the message about hard work and sacrifice has been greatly diluted for the past 40 years. There are still many parents and teachers doing an excellent job of helping kids understand the importance of a solid work ethic, but too many of our young people (including many young adults) aren't getting the message. I saw it in school and many of my friends in business saw it in the workplace. There have been countless studies done in recent years that tell us what we already knew: many of our young people are growing up with a sense of entitlement and are about ten years slower than previous generations in accepting full adult responsibilities.

"There's a quick and easy way"

"You can have it all, and you can have it now"

How many times have you heard these two statements? Probably more than you can count. My generation never heard

them, but our young people today have been bombarded
with them constantly since they were born. They're two of
the advertising industry's favorite, and most effective, ways
to get people to buy things. Our kids hear them so often that
it registers in their subconscious minds that this is how life
works. Students heard otherwise in my classroom. Here are
three of what became known as "Urbanisms" (there were
many others):

1. **Nothing important was ever attained the "quick and
   easy" way.**

2. **No one can have it all, and no one can have it all now.**

3. **There's no substitute for hard work.**
   (This is the title of Chapter 13 in *Life's Greatest Lessons*)

Is there any good news here? Yes. The importance of
developing a strong work ethic *can* be taught and it *can* be
learned. Here's an example: Several years ago, while I was still
in the classroom, Tim, one of my former students dropped
by for a visit. He'd been out of high school for more than ten
years. We caught up on each other's lives, and then I asked
him the same question I ask all my former students: "What's
something you remember from your days as a student in my
class?" He didn't hesitate for a second. He smiled and said,
"Two things. One, life is hard. Two, we reap what we sow." He
added, "And they go together." I think I said something like
"Hallelujah!," and gave him a high five.

I tell this story, not to make myself look like the world's
greatest teacher, (I'm sure there are some students who don't
remember *anything*) but to point out that most kids remember life lessons more than they remember academic lessons.
Tim and hundreds of other students have told me over the
years that my lessons on making choices (the seven covered
in this section) were among the most valuable things they

learned. Next time you hear "quick and easy" and "you can have it all," just remind yourself that it doesn't work that way. Tell yourself this instead: **Achievement is the result of hard work and sacrifice. We reap what we sow.**

One of the most meaningful words in the dictionary

Achievement is defined in most dictionaries as the completion of a task or the attainment of a goal through one's own efforts. While looking it up in several dictionaries and thesaurus, I compiled a list of words that are often associated with *achievement:*

work	exertion	strive	labor	endeavor
diligence	energy	sacrifice	effort	perseverance
excellence	character	enthusiasm	success	self-discipline

The challenge

At the beginning of every school year I read my mission statement as a teacher out loud to my students, then posted it on the wall. It was not only a mission statement, it was a promise to my students. It contained several parts. Among them were: I would treat them with respect, I would be prepared each day with a meaningful lesson, I would maintain high standards, and that I wasn't afraid to make my students work. The last part of my mission statement contained these seven words:

"I will *always* give you my best."

Then I posed a question that caught them off guard. I asked, "Can I expect you to give me *your* best each time you come to my class?" Almost all of them thought the teacher giving his best was far different than the students giving their best. Why? "Because you get paid, and we don't." My response was (with a smile), "Not true." I carefully explained that I got paid for doing my job—teaching—whether I put in the minimum or the maximum effort. Now they were starting to get it. I told them I couldn't live with myself if I didn't give them the best I had. Self-respect is one of the rewards of always putting forth your best effort. A few more are a sense of accomplishment, earning the respect of others, getting the best possible results, and the character development that comes when we consistently work hard.

I wasn't going to convince them in one short discussion to give 100 percent effort in every endeavor every day of their lives, but I did get them thinking. I also challenged them to give it a try: go one day in which you give your best in everything you do. I asked them, "Why would you ever want to give less than your best? Life is so much more rewarding when you do." I also asked them to look at a new sign I was putting up in the classroom, and to give me an answer after they'd thought it about it for a day.

WHY NOT YOUR BEST?

The next day, before I asked them if anyone had an answer for me, Ryan, a senior, raised his hand. He said, "Dr. Urban, I know why you asked us that question and put that sign up. You asked us because there *is* no good answer. There's never a reason for not giving your best." Talk about making a teacher happy! The truth is, there *isn't* a good reason to ever give less than our best. Plain and simple, hard workers live more rewarding lives.

About 12 years later I saw Ryan at a wedding of one of his classmates. He had finished college, gotten married, and was well into his career. I asked him if he remembered that day in class when I put up the **WHY NOT YOUR BEST?** sign. He said, "Absolutely! And I *do* give my best all the time. I don't succeed in everything I do, but at least I know I gave it my best shot. Life really is better when we give the best we have. And as you always said, 'We reap what we sow.'"

I wish every student I ever taught "got it" like Ryan did. But I do get reminded often by both former students and their parents that learning about the importance of a good work ethic was one of the most valuable things they learned in high school. And almost all of them add that hard work is an important part of good character.

What successful people have told us about the rewards of hard work

Work hard and become a leader; be lazy and never succeed.

> —*King Solomon, Proverbs 12:24*

The best prize life offers is the chance to work hard at work worth doing.

> —*Theodore Roosevelt, President*

I learned that the only way you are going to get anywhere in life is to work hard at it. Whether you're a musician, a writer, an athlete, or a businessman, there's no getting around it. Work hard and you win; don't and you lose.

> —*Bruce Jenner, Olympic Gold Medalist*

Success is 1 percent inspiration and 99 percent perspiration.

> —*Thomas Edison, inventor*

I've got a theory that if you give 100 percent all of the time, somehow things will work out in the end.

—*Larry Bird, Hall of Fame basketball player*

When I was young, I observed that nine out of ten things I did were failures. So I did ten times more work.

—*George Bernard Shaw, Nobel Prize winner in Literature*

The price of success is hard work, dedication to the job at hand, and the determination that whether we win or lose, we have applied the best of ourselves to the task at hand.

—*Vince Lombardi, Hall of Fame football coach*

Personal Notes

Personal Notes

chapter 10 *You are what you are because of what goes into your mind*

You can change who you are by changing what goes into your mind.

—*David J. Abbott, M.D.*

Who and what puts things into our minds?

Every day of our lives we receive literally thousands of messages. They come from a wide variety of sources, and can be good, neutral, or bad. Let's look at some of the primary sources of our daily input:

Parents/family	Friends	Newspapers
Magazines	Books	Television
Music	Movies	School
Radio	Internet	Video games
Faith	Advertising	Mail: letters, e-mail, texts

There isn't any research that shows which of the above sources send the most messages or have the most influence. That's because everyone is different. One person might watch

TV for eight hours a day, while another plays video games for the same amount of time. One person might spend six hours a day reading, while another surfs the Internet for the same amount of time. One person might spend four hours a day sending and receiving e-mails and text messages, while another spends the same amount of time socializing in person with friends. These are all choices. Now think of all the choices within these choices. For example:

- What does the person watch on TV?

- What does the person read?

- Which video games does the person play?

- What is the person viewing on the Internet?

- Who does the person socialize with? What do they talk about?

- What kinds of messages are sent and received via e-mail and texts?

An exercise that's of great value to any person from 8 to 80 is to take a closer look at the sources that are putting information into his or her mind. For instance, go back to the sources listed on the first page of this chapter. Rank them from 1 to 15 in terms of the amount of time you spend with each on an average non-school or non-workday. Then ask yourself these two questions:

1. Is the input from these sources good, neutral, or bad?

2. Do I need to make some changes regarding the sources of my input?

Do you let any garbage in?

Please turn back and look at the title of this chapter again. It's actually a quote by a man who's had a positive influence on the lives of millions, including this author. His name is Zig Ziglar, and he's 86 as I write this. He's best known as a "motivational speaker" and author. I respect and admire him because of his wisdom, his uplifting message, his humor, his reverence, his kindness, his sincerity, and his special ability to touch people's hearts.

Of the many reasons I admire him, you'll note that I mentioned his *wisdom* first. He has a down-to-earth, common sense, straightforward way of looking at the complexities of life and reducing them to the essentials. This is what wisdom is. His statement that, "You are what you are because of what goes into your mind," ranks (in this author's opinion) among the wisest things ever said. It's not far behind "We reap what we sow."

Many years ago when I heard Mr. Ziglar speak in Oakland, California, he asked the audience a question: "Would you allow a person carrying a large bag of trash to walk into your living room and dump it all there?" Then he hesitated for a few moments while his question sank in with the audience. I was thinking, as were hundreds of others, "Of course not. Why would he even ask such a silly question?" But he was obviously setting up his main point. A few minutes later, he said, "Please raise your hand if the answer is NO." All the hands went up.

Then he asked another question: "Would you let anyone dump trash into your mind?" Again, there was a pause. He just wanted the people in the audience to think about both questions and the point he was making. He didn't ask for a show of hands after the second question because he, and all the rest of us, knew the answer. It was YES. We *do* let people and popular culture dump trash into our minds on a daily basis, but it happens more subtly than watching a person dump a load of garbage in our living room.

It's true that you can't screen out 100 percent of the thousands of messages you receive each day. But it's also true that we *can* screen out a high percentage of them. Even more important, you can choose not only the source of the input, but the content of the input. Since you are what you are because of what goes into your mind, let me ask you a few questions:

Do you make good choices regarding your daily input?
Do you allow anyone to dump garbage into your mind?

G.I.G.O.

GIGO is an old term which comes from the early days of computer science and communication technology. Basically, it means that if you put wrong or nonsensical information into your computer, you will get wrong or nonsensical information out of it. Garbage In, Garbage Out. Now apply this principle to the human mind. If you allow negative, filthy, mean-spirited, and sleazy information into your mind (Garbage In) on a regular basis, you will become a person whose values, words, and actions are negative, filthy, mean-spirited, and sleazy (Garbage Out).

Here's an example—A person occupies his or her time on a Saturday by doing the following: plays four hours of violent video games in which the goal is to kill as many persons and blow up as many objects as possible; spends two hours reading *The National Enquirer* (exaggerated, misleading, and often untrue information about the lives of celebrities); watches pornography on the Internet for two hours; spends two hours in conversation with friends who are angry, negative, disrespectful, and filthy-mouthed. That's ten hours of Garbage In. If this person does these things on a regular basis, how do think he or she thinks, talks, and acts? Both research and common sense tell us that it will be Garbage Out.

Another example—How does an innocent and lovable ten year old boy or girl become a savage terrorist at age 16? The answer is that his or her mind is polluted on a daily basis for six years with false, fanatic, and hateful information by political and religious zealots. Garbage In, Garbage Out.

Now let's change the *G's* in GIGO. Let's change *Garbage* to *Good,* as in Good In, Good Out. If you allow positive, clean, kind, and uplifting information into your mind (Good In) on a regular basis, you will become a person whose values, words, and actions are positive, clean, kind, and uplifting (Good Out).

Here's an example—A person occupies his or her time on a Saturday by doing the following: spends two hours reading books by Hal Urban. Just kidding. What I really meant to write was "reading books by any author that are uplifting and help build character"; devotes two hours to reading newspapers and magazines for the purpose of becoming better informed about what's going on in the world, including sports, business, and entertainment; watches a two-hour movie on TV that is clean, upbeat, and funny (I think there a few left); goes on the Internet for two hours for the purpose of learning; spends two hours with family and friends talking about meaningful and positive things while enjoying each other's company. That's ten hours of Good In. If this person does these things on a regular basis, how do you think he or she thinks, talks, and acts? Both research and common sense tell us it will be Good Out.

Another example—How does an innocent and lovable ten year old boy or girl become kind, hard-working, and admired at age 16? The answer is that his or her mind is filled on a daily basis for six years with true and uplifting information by parents, teachers, and friends. Good In, Good Out.

Pollute your mind or nourish it?
The choice is yours

Let me conclude this chapter by saying that the danger of polluting a mind is not in the sources of input themselves. I happen to love movies, the Internet, a wide variety of reading materials, TV programs, and socializing with friends. But I also love and treasure the mind God gave me. It's the well-spring of my life, as is yours. Isn't it wonderful that we have the freedom and the power to use technology and the media to nourish our minds and help us lead healthy lives?

What goes into a mind comes out in a life!

—*Addison County Readers, Inc.,*
Middlebury, Vermont

PERSONAL NOTES

_____

_____

_____

_____

_____

_____

_____

_____

_____

_____

_____

_____

_____

_____

_____

_____

_____

Personal Notes

chapter 11 *Your body is a lifetime vehicle; it requires care and maintenance*

Take care of your body. It's the only place you have to live.

—*Jim Rohn*

A paradox

A paradox is a seemingly true statement that leads to a contradiction or situation which seems to be the opposite.

First, the true statement. This is something I wrote in 1990 in *Life's Greatest Lessons*: "At no time in our history have we been more aware of the benefits of caring for the body. We have knowledge about nutrition and exercise that wasn't available as recently as ten years ago. And we've experienced a genuine fitness explosion. People of all ages are paying closer attention to what goes into their bodies and are becoming more physically active. And they're living longer, healthier, and more productive lives."

Second, the contradiction. While millions of people are still caring for their bodies, we have the opposite occurring at the same time. In other words, we have more kids and adults who are overweight, obese, physically inactive, and out of shape than ever before. How can this be when we have so much valuable information about living a healthy lifestyle? Pure logic tells me that there can only be three reasons:

1. Ignorance (not knowing)—this is particularly true of children who grow up in families who are uninformed, eat unhealthy food, and don't exercise. They become socialized into this style of living and it becomes a habit. This is why schools are finally paying more attention to health matters and teaching about nutrition and exercise.

2. Laziness—this is true of people who know they should maintain a healthier diet and know they should exercise more, but they choose to do neither. A common phrase that comes from them is: "I don't need the 'health cops' telling me what I should and should not eat, and what I should and should not do with my body."

3. Lack of self-control—You might recall that I called self-control the "master skill of life" back in Chapter 3. It has everything to do with living a healthy lifestyle. Saying *no* to one thing (unhealthy food) often means saying *yes* to something more important (a healthy body).

Which side of this paradox are you on? The nutrition and exercise side or the unhealthy lifestyle side? You make the choice every day.

Your lifetime vehicle

Our body is a machine for living. It is organized for that; it is its nature. Let life go on it.

—*Leo Tolstoy*

Some people reading this aren't old enough to drive yet, let alone own a car. Others reading it have owned several cars. Let's assume, just for this moment, that everyone reading this is 16 years old and about to get their first car. And let's assume that for some unknown reason, there's a law that says each person is entitled to own only one car in a lifetime. If you live to be 90, this car has to last you for 74 years. If this was the case, how would you treat that car from day one? I'm guessing that, knowing it has to last you for the rest of your life, you would take very good care of it. You'd be careful how you drive it, you'd keep it clean, you'd be sure to have it serviced regularly, you'd keep it tuned, and you'd put the right fuel into it.

I'm sure you see where I'm headed with this, because this chapter is about the body as a vehicle. Now let's assume that on the day you're born, your Creator says to you, "The body I'm giving you is the vehicle that will carry you through life. But please remember that each person only gets one. Take good care of it because it has to last you a lifetime." Unlike the made-up law in the above paragraph about getting only one car during your lifetime, this law about getting only one body is for real.

The point is simple: take the best possible care of your body. If you do, you'll be more healthy both physically and mentally, you'll be happier, you'll feel better about yourself, you'll achieve more, and you'll live longer. But keep in mind that it's hard work to get and stay in top physical condition. There's no "quick and easy" way to do it. You need two important tools:

1. Self-control is the master skill of life (Chapter 3)— This means you're in charge of what does and does not go into your body. And it means you're in charge of what you do (exercise) and don't do (be a couch potato) with your body.

2. Achievement is the result of hard work (Chapter 9)— This means that having a healthy body is one of life's most important achievements. Not because your body is the most essential thing in life, but because it's the vehicle that *carries* what's most essential.

> Your body is precious, as it houses your mind and
> spirit.
>
> — Norman Vincent Peale

What goes into your body? Is it toxic or nourishing?

> Our food should be our medicine and our medicine
> should be our food.
>
> —Hippocrates (460-370 BC)

With so much valuable information about what to eat and drink and what not to eat and drink available to us, it's hardly necessary for me to go into great detail here. So let me make a suggestion for the Personal Notes pages at the end of this chapter. Turn on your computer, go to Google, then type in "ten healthiest foods." You'll find several such lists by trustworthy organizations such as the Mayo Clinic and the Live Strong Foundation. Find some healthy foods that you like, write ten of them down, and make them a regular part of your diet. Also do a Google search on the "ten unhealthiest foods." Write down the ones you consume most often, and make a sincere effort to cut down on or eliminate them from your diet. Don't be surprised if you find soft drinks, hamburgers, potato chips, french fries and doughnuts on those lists. Alcohol, drugs, and tobacco are discussed in Chapter 16.

Let me close out this topic with advice that every doctor on the planet would give you: DRINK A LOT OF WATER!

Google "benefits of drinking water," and you'll understand why it's called the elixir (miraculous substance) of life. It's the healthiest thing you can put into your body. And it's cheap.

> *To eat is a necessity, but to eat intelligently is an art.*
> —*Francois de La Rochefoucauld*

What do you <u>do</u> with your body? Is it toxic or nourishing?

> *Those who think they have not time for bodily exercise will sooner or later have to find time for illness.*
> —*Edward Stanley*

As with the food and drink issue, I want to start with the toxic things people do to their bodies beyond putting the wrong substances into them.

However, this is a completely different way of damaging your body. When you put any substance into it, you're consciously aware of what you're doing. You go to McDonald's and see a Big Mac, fries, and a coke on the menu board. You order them and you eat them.

Toxic activity (or lack of it)—Now comes the point about damaging your body by what you *do* (or *don't do*) with it beyond eating and drinking. The number one way is "sitting around." In other words, sitting way too much, as in most of every day. You could be watching TV, playing video games, surfing the Internet, writing, reading, even working. There's nothing wrong with any of these activities, but if you "sit around" too much, without getting any exercise, you're doing serious damage to your body.

"Use it or lose it" is a frequently heard phrase that contains a lot of common sense and wisdom. It could apply to many aspects of life, but in this case it's being applied to the human body. Remember what Tolstoy said: the body is "a machine for living." Machines require both usage and care. What happens to a machine that's never used, one that just sits? It eventually corrodes and becomes unusable. This is what happens to a body when it doesn't get enough exercise: muscles atrophy, the heart and lungs weaken, strength is diminished, weight increases, energy level decreases, blood circulation worsens, bad moods and depression often set in, and other diseases are more likely to occur.

Nourishing activity for the body—The good news is that there are countless ways (most of them fun) in which people can get the proper amount of exercise. A few examples are team sports, exercise classes, walking, hiking, running, biking, working out at a gym, swimming, and other water sports. The beauty is that all of these except team sports and exercise classes can be done either alone or with other people. There's often a rewarding social dimension to exercising.

Here are some of the great rewards of keeping your body moving in healthy ways: it burns calories and helps keep your weight down; it strengthens your heart—the most important muscle/organ in your body; it helps people look better and feel better about themselves; it promotes good health and helps ward off disease; it increases energy levels; it makes people happy, as regular exercise produces endorphins, which are chemicals in the brain that produce good feelings.

Lack of activity destroys the good condition of every human being, while movement and methodical physical exercise save it and preserve it.

—Plato (429-347 BC)

We should respect the sun, not worship it

I was one of those California sun worshipers for many years. The reason was simple: being tan was cool. I worked in the sun, played in the sun, and lay in the sun for hours and hours. I never wore a hat or sunglasses and rarely put sunscreen on. The result? A cool tan when I was younger and skin cancer when I got older. I've had five surgical procedures for both melanoma and basil cell cancer. I was lucky. The melanoma cancer cells didn't get into my blood stream and cause additional damage or a premature death. It *has* happened to millions of people.

This doesn't mean that you should avoid the sun entirely. In fact some exposure to the sun is necessary. It's our main source of Vitamin D, which protects us in many ways. Sunny days also lift our spirits. But because of my own scary and painful lesson resulting from too much unprotected sun exposure, I felt a need to include a warning and some advice in a chapter about taking good care of our bodies. The advice is simple: avoid prolonged periods in the sun, and when you are in it, do what I *didn't* do—wear a hat, wear sunglasses, and put sunscreen on that has a high protection number. Avoid skin cancer and the premature wrinkling of your skin. Enjoy the sun, but respect it.

Suggestion: go to skincancer.org and read what the Skin Cancer Foundation has to say. You'll be glad you did.

Habits are the key to healthy living

The title of Chapter 6 in *Life's Greatest Lessons* is, "Habits are the key to all success." It applies to every aspect of life, as it's been proven that we're "creatures of habit." Some psychologists believe that up to 95 percent of our behavior is formed as a result of habit. As Charles C. Noble wrote back in the 1800s, "First we make our habits, then our habits make us."

Keep in mind that this maxim applies to what we drink, what we eat, and what we do and don't do with our lifetime vehicles.

> *As I see it, every day you do one of two things:*
> *build health or produce disease in yourself.*
>
> —*Adelle Davis*

PERSONAL NOTES

Personal Notes

chapter 12 *Money is important; learning how to manage it is more important*

> *Your money is a huge part of your life. It can determine what you can do and where you can go. Learning how to manage your money the right way is an important step toward taking control of your life.*
>
> *—Mapping Your Future website*

The two keys to financial security

I was born in the early 1940s, which means I came into the world during The Great Depression (1929-1945). It also means that my parents lived through this entire period as young adults. Because they survived hard financial times, they wanted me to understand the value of money and the basics of handling it successfully. My parents were neither rich nor educated. My dad was a ninth grade dropout who became an ironworker. My mom graduated from high school and went to work in a bank. After marrying my dad she became a stay-at-home mom until I was in the seventh grade, then went to work as a secretary. They didn't make a lot of money, but they provided a comfortable middle class lifestyle for their family. How did they do this? They handled their money wisely. And they taught me well, starting when I was about ten years old. I learned that there were two simple keys to becoming financially secure:

1. Learn how to save

> *There is absolutely no time better to save money than when you're young.*
>
> —Warren Buffett

I heard early and often from my parents that one of the biggest mistakes people make with their money is not saving enough of it, if any. I still remember going to the local savings and loan bank with my mom to open my first personal savings account. I was taught to save at least ten percent of all the money I took in, whether it was from gifts or income from a job. I was also urged to save even more than ten percent whenever I received unexpected money, such as an extra large gift, a bonus at work, or overtime pay.

It didn't take long to fully understand what my parents meant when they said people didn't save enough. I got some good summer jobs when I was a kid, and saved well more than ten percent of it. It was fun to watch that money pile up and earn interest on top of it. But of all my friends, only Terry had a regular savings plan and financial goals like I did. He had been taught the same thing by his parents. The others spent every penny they took in on the latest this or that, and none of them had any personal savings by the time they graduated from high school.

When I was in college it was the same thing. We all went home for the summer, got good jobs (they were plentiful then), and earned a lot of money. I was particularly lucky to work in the lumber yards every summer. It was hard physical labor, but the pay was outstanding. I was earning more than eight times what the minimum wage was at the time. I saved more than half of it. Terry also made good money in the summer, and he told me that he saved more than half. Our other friends? They continued to spend every penny that came in, and graduated from college without any personal savings. They said they'd start saving for a home after they got their first full-time job. My parents had impressed upon me that I should have enough money to make a down payment on a home by the time I finished college. I did. I was 25 when I completed my Master's degree, and bought my first home that summer.

Here are a few facts that prove what my parents told me was, and still is, true: **one of the biggest mistakes people make with their money is not saving enough of it, if any.**

- Compared to all other advanced nations, Americans save the least.

- More than 40 percent of individuals in the U.S. do not have savings.

- Among those who *do* save, the amount has declined dramatically. In the 1960s people saved eleven percent of their income. It was down to five percent in the 1990s, and down to less than three percent in the 2000s.

- The average American family carries more than $9,000 worth of credit card debt.

- Personal bankruptcy grew more than 350% between the years 1980-2010.

- More than 40 percent of American families spend more money than they bring in each year.

Any successful money manager would give you the same advice that Warren Buffet gives in the quote at the beginning of this section: **start saving now!** While it's best to save at a young age, it's never too late to start. The key is doing it on a regular basis.

> *Learning to save money is the first step toward achieving your financial goals.*
>
> —*Personal Finance Insights*

2. Learn how to spend money

> *Your personal spending habits are the key to being successful with money. Learning to save and being a smart shopper are the things that lead to wealth.*
>
> —*Mark Cuban*

The other important thing I learned from my parents about handling money was what they called the "Don't Buy Rules":

- Don't buy anything you can't afford.

- Don't buy anything that's not necessary.

- Don't buy anything to impress others.

- Don't buy anything on impulse.

- Don't buy anything until you've found the best price.

Let me give you a true-to-life example of a person who bought something in violation of all five of my parents' rules. A few years ago I stopped at a gas station. While I was filling up my inexpensive but reliable Nissan Sentra , I couldn't help notice the beautiful new Chevrolet Camaro convertible next to me. While admiring it, I realized that the young woman filling it up was one of my former students. She had graduated from high school only two years earlier, so we both recognized each other immediately. After greeting me warmly she filled me in on her life. She got a job right after graduating and moved into an apartment with one of her girlfriends. She said, "I really wanted to be independent."

I said, "You must be doing well. That's a beautiful car you're driving." Big mistake. I thought the compliment would make her happy, but it had the opposite effect. Her smile turned to a frown, as she responded, "Oh, Dr. Urban, buying this car was the biggest mistake of my life." She went on to explain that the Camaro had always been her dream car, and she "just had to have it." Well, now she had it, but it wasn't such a great thing. Here are the "don't buy" rules she broke:

1. She couldn't afford it. Her monthly car payment was swallowing her.

2. It wasn't necessary. She said, "I should have bought a practical car like you did." Score one for my little Sentra.

3. She bought it to impress her friends. They all thought it was "way cool."

4. She bought it on impulse. She said she went to the showroom only to "look" at the car because she knew she couldn't afford it. But a slick salesman sold her both the car and a bad loan. Mainly because he knew that she "just had to have it."

5. She didn't shop for the best price. Had she gone to two or three dealers she would have either found a much lower price and better loan or realized that she was getting in over her head.

It was a truly sad conversation because she grew more upset as we talked. She said in great frustration, "I just don't know what I'm going to do." Under the circumstances I couldn't say, "Gee, it was great seeing you!" The truth is, our meeting was a bit of a downer, and I felt sorry for her. She had made a big and costly mistake. The saddest part of all of this is that these types of purchases (cars and a lot of other things) happen thousands of times every day, all over the country, by people of all ages. Why? Because they never learned how to handle their money. They never learned to develop wise personal spending habits.

> *There is more justification in rational saving*
> *than in irrational spending.*
>
> —P. T. Barnum

Jack and Jill—two examples of saving and spending

1. Jack—"Money is for having fun"

Jack was born into a middle class family in 1980. His mother and father both worked. But they never saved and never taught their son anything about handling money. Between the ages of 10-15 he received about $400 a year—$2400 total—in gifts from relatives, mostly from his grandparents. He spent all of it on cool things. He got a nice job when he was 16, and between working part-time during school and full-time in the summer, he made about $7,200 a year—$21,600 total—until he graduated from high school at 18. Even though his parents were paying for his necessities up to that time, he still spent all of his income (after taxes) on cool things.

After high school he got a full-time job in his uncle's successful produce market. He started out at $30,000 per year, worked hard, and got a nice bonus and raise at the end of each year. Between the ages of 18-25 he averaged $35,000 per year—a total of $280,000. He paid his income taxes, and then spent all the rest of the money on his apartment, hot cars, a monster TV and sound system, and every new electronic toy that came out. He also partied a lot. His income couldn't quite support his lifestyle, so he took out a big (and expensive) loan on his car, and paid for most of the other things with credit cards. He made the minimum payment each month, so he was charged an enormous amount in interest.

When a couple of his friends told Jack that he should handle his money more carefully, he said, "Money is for having fun." By the time he was 25 he had nothing in savings or in a retirement fund, and was more than $22,000 in debt.

2. Jill—"Money, if handled properly, is a resource for a good life."

Jill was born into a middle class family in 1980. Her mother and father both worked. They handled their money carefully, and saved a minimum of ten percent of their income every year. They taught Jill when she was young how to handle money. So did Jill's grandparents. Between the ages of 10-15 she received about $400 a year—$2400 total—in gifts from relatives, mostly from her grandparents. Because she listened to her "financial advisors," and because her parents were supporting her, she saved $1800 of it. Her grandfather invested it for her in conservative and safe stocks and bonds.

Jill got a nice job when she was 16, and between working part-time during school and full-time in the summer, she made $7,200 a year—$21,600 total—until she graduated from high school at 18. Because her parents were taking care of most of her financial needs, she saved (after paying income taxes) another $12,000. She asked her grandfather to invest it again for her because she enjoyed looking at her monthly statements. Her money grew.

After high school she got a full-time job in her uncle's successful insurance company. She started out at $30,000 per year, worked hard, and got a nice bonus and raise at the end of each year. Between the ages of 18-25 she averaged $35,000 per year—a total of $280,000. She paid her income taxes, lived in a modest apartment with a good friend, drove an inexpensive and economical car (probably a Nissan Sentra), and practiced sound spending habits while still living comfortably. She never got a credit card. She paid for things with cash, her debit card, or with a check. Some of her friends urged her to loosen up with her money so she could "have more things and have more fun." She told them she had everything she needed and was "having fun" watching her money grow. She told them, "Money, if handled properly, is a resource for a good life." Her grandfather had told her that.

She saved as much as she could. Her goal was to save $600 per month, and she not only achieved it, but was able to add more from time to time. This means she saved $7,200 or more each year, or $58,200 by the time she was 25. This is in addition to the $1,800 she saved when she was younger. So her total savings by the time she was 25 was $60,000. Again, she had her grandfather invest it safely and conservatively. She earned about five percent each year on her investments, so over the years she made an additional $23,000. At age 25 Jill had $83,000 saved and had no debt.

Jack—Born in 1980, he brought in $304,000 in gifts and income between the ages of 10-25. In 2005 he had no savings and was in debt $22,000.

Jill—Born in 1980, she brought in $304,000 in gifts and income between the ages of 10-25. In 2005 she had $83,000 saved and had no debt.

Isn't it amazing what saving and spending wisely will accomplish?

The Millionaire Next Door

The heading above is the title of a best-selling book written in 1996 by Thomas Stanley and William Danko. It's not about flashy get-rich-quick schemes or about secrets that will turn you into a mega-millionaire. It's about everyday people who learn to handle their money wisely, and then plug away year after year. Some of them become wealthy, and all of them become financially secure. This is the way the book is described by Travis Morien, a highly successful Australian financial planner: "It involves the slow process of . . . saving up your money instead of spending it, budgeting down to the last cent, investing carefully, and seeking out good advice when necessary."

Four reminders that apply to handling money

1. Self-control is the master skill of life—Chapter 3
2. Achievement is the result of hard work—Chapter 9
3. Habits are the key to all success—Chapter 6 in *Life's Greatest Lessons*
4. We reap what we sow—Chapter 2

Be industrious and frugal, and you will be rich.
        —Benjamin Franklin

Personal Notes

PERSONAL NOTES

part
2 *A Recap*

Choices, choices, choices

Let me reinforce something I wrote at the beginning of this section about understanding the importance of making good choices:

1. We were given a free will—the power to make choices.
2. We make hundreds of choices every day.
3. If we don't make our own choices, someone else will make them for us.
4. The choices we make will determine the quality of our lives. In other words, we reap what we sow.

Seven choices you make every day

1. You choose your **ATTITUDE**. It's your control center in both good and bad times.
2. You choose whether to be **HONEST** or not in all circumstances.
3. You choose whether you'll be **KIND** to others no matter who comes into contact with you.
4. You choose how hard you'll **WORK** no matter what responsibilities you have.
5. You choose what goes into your **MIND**. You are what you are because of what you let into it.
6. You choose what you put into your **BODY** and what you do with it.
7. You choose whether to save **MONEY** or not, and you choose how to spend it.

You have brains in your head.
You have feet in your shoes.
You can steer yourself any direction you choose.

—*Dr. Seuss,* ***Oh! The Places You'll Go!***

part
3 *Eight Suggestions for Making Life More Meaningful*

Life is a succession of lessons which must be lived to be understood.

—Ralph Waldo Emerson

The striving to find meaning in one's life is the primary motivational force in man.

—Viktor Frankl

Our souls are not hungry for fame, comfort, wealth, or power. Those rewards create almost as many problems as they solve. Our souls hunger for meaning, for the sense that we have figured out how to live so that our lives matter, so that the world will be at least a little bit different for our having passed through it.

—Rabbi Harold Kushner

The insights and words of the three great men quoted above have stated the importance of learning to find meaning in our lives much better than this author ever could. I hope the next eight chapters help you understand that the happiest people in the world are the ones who find this meaning. While it may differ from person to person, those who find it enjoy fuller and richer lives.

chapter

13 *Positive words have powerful results*

Words have the power to destroy or heal. When words are both true and kind, they can change our world.

—Buddha, 563-483 BC

How kind words can change our world

Kind words can be short and easy to speak, but their echoes are truly endless.

—Mother Teresa, 1910-1997

Several years ago I was speaking at a large conference of realtors in Florida. One of the main speakers was Phil McGraw, better known as "Dr. Phil" to the followers of his popular TV show. Because I wasn't speaking until later, I decided to sit in on his presentation, which was outstanding. He said something that day that fascinated me, made me think, and has stuck in my mind ever since. He said that most people have at least five "Pivotal Persons" come into their lives. He described them as people, other than family members, who can appear in our lives at any time, and dramatically change it for the better. I immediately asked myself the same question everyone else in the audience was asking themselves: "Who are the five people in my life? Who, outside of my family, have had the greatest impact on my life?" It was surprisingly easy to answer. I came up with five names in seconds. The first one was Tim Hansel. I've written about Tim in previous books, and I'll probably write about him in future books. He had that great of an impact. How did he do it? With kind, loving, positive, uplifting, encouraging, inspiring, and life-enhancing words.

Tim and I were both colleagues and friends for many years, and I'll always remember him as one of the most influential persons in my life. One of the things I noticed shortly after meeting him was that he never said anything negative. In other words, he didn't swear, gossip, complain, or put people down. Everything that came out of his mouth was positive.

I asked him one day while we were eating lunch if there was a story behind his all-positive-no-negative talk. He said with a big smile, "Yeah, there sure is." He said his parents passed on their personal motto to him, which was, "Always have something good to say!" I asked him to explain how it came about. He said he had been very lucky. Both of his parents were kind, upbeat, and funny, and they used their words accordingly. Tim said he was about ten when his parents taught him to memorize a verse from the Bible:

> Do not let any unwholesome talk come out of your mouths, but only what is helpful for building others up according to their needs, that it may benefit those who listen.
>
> —Ephesians 4:29

Tim didn't just memorize it, he lived it. He didn't just preach it, he practiced it. In the opening quotes for this chapter, Buddha says kind words can change our world, and Mother Teresa says that the echoes of kind words are truly endless. That's the effect Tim's words had, not only on me, but on his students, colleagues, friends, associates, and even strangers. He always had a smile on his face, and he always had something good to say. He had a special knack for finding the best in other people, and telling them what he found. He affirmed people, he brought out the best in them, he enhanced their lives. How? With positive words.

Tim died in December of 2008 after a long illness. I flew down to southern California for his service. It was truly a celebration of life! There were hundreds of people in attendance, and many were given the opportunity to speak. Their comments, and mine, could be summed up in four words: "He changed my life." How? By living up to his personal motto: "Always have something good to say." I wish everyone could have a Tim Hansel come into their lives. He would show how positive words have powerful results, not only on the person sending them, but on the person receiving them.

> *Words go into the body. So they can cause us to be*
> *well and hopeful and happy and high-energy and*
> *wondrous and funny and cheerful …*
>
> —*Maya Angelou*

Toxic or nourishing?

> *Reckless words can pierce like a sword, but the*
> *tongue of the wise brings healing.*
>
> —*King Solomon, Proverbs 12:18*

I taught a unit on the power of words to my students at both the high school and at the university every year. They agreed with me that all of our words fall into one of three categories: positive, neutral, negative. By *neutral*, I mean the words we use to exchange information. It could be me teaching about Benjamin Franklin or it could be you getting directions to a restaurant. Since they *are* neutral, there's no need to discuss them here. But there *is* a need to discuss the other two types of words. They often make a lasting impact either for good or for bad. In my classes we called the negative words "toxic," as in poisoning the atmosphere. The positive words were called "nourishing," as in stimulating and promoting growth in the atmosphere.

I wrote the word TOXIC in big letters on the left side of the chalkboard, and the word NOURISHING on the other side. I said, "Now tell me what you *don't* want to hear and what you *do* want to hear." They gave me a long list of each. One class in 1998 gave me 30 of each, so we gave them nicknames of "The Dirty Thirty" and "The Thoughtful Thirty." I don't want to list all of them here, but do want to list the ones that my students found to be the most toxic and the most nourishing.

TOXIC	NOURISHING
Put-downs	Compliments
Gossip	Friendly greetings
Complaining	Encouragement
Filthy words	Caring words
Rude words	Expressing thanks

Which of the above do you most want to hear? More important, which of the above do you most frequently use? Remember Chapter 8? The title is "Every act of kindness makes the world a better place, and you a better person." Saying something complimentary or caring or encouraging to another person is, indeed, an act of kindness. It *will* make the world a better place, and it *will* make you a better person. Remember what the previous section (seven chapters) of this book was about? It was about the choices we make every day. Since kindness is a choice, then every word that comes out of our mouths is also a choice. My suggestion? Adopt my friend Tim's motto: "Always have something good to say." It would make him happy, it will make someone else happy, and it will make you happy.

What a great student most remembered

You cannot receive a sincere compliment without feeling better ... and just as important, you cannot give a sincere compliment without feeling better yourself.

—*Zig Ziglar*

During my many years in the classroom I taught more than 9,000 students. Obviously, I don't remember all of them. But I remember many, and still have regular contact. A few of them were so special they had a life-long impact on me, even though it was supposed to be the other way around. One of them was Bill. He was blessed with all kinds of energy, intelligence, talent, and imagination. More important, he was incredibly kind and sensitive to the needs of others. I was literally in awe of him.

He was in one of my 12th grade Psychology classes. Every teacher knows that there are some classes that are an absolute joy to teach. This was one of many in my career, and Bill was a major contributor. During the first week of the semester we did the toxic-nourishing words exercise. While we were discussing it after the kids gave me their lists, I commented that all people should try to be more affirming with their words. Some of the students didn't know what "affirming" meant. For the purpose of simplicity, I said it means to "build people up instead of tearing them down."

Everyone in the class agreed, but Bill had a reservation. He asked, "Won't it come across as phony? Won't most people think you're trying to 'butter them up' so you can get something from them?" His points were well taken. Most people *aren't* used to being on the receiving end of affirming words, so they become suspicious of your motives. We had a good class discussion about the importance of being sincere. Bill told me a couple of days later that he'd been thinking a lot about why more people don't use affirming language. "It's so easy," he said. And then he added, "And everyone wins."

Late that spring Bill graduated with honors and went on to Yale University. Four years later, as he was about to again graduate with honors, he wrote me a letter that I'll always cherish. I quoted Mother Teresa earlier. She said kind words have echoes that are "truly endless." The echoes of Bill's letter are exactly that. In it, he told me that the lesson on affirming language was one of the most valuable things he learned in high school, even though he was a little skeptical at first. He said the lesson helped him in four ways:

1. It increased his awareness of the power of words, good or bad.
2. It helped him look for the good in other people, and to tell them what he found. He said, "I always have something good to say."
3. It became easy and natural to affirm others after he had done it regularly for a few weeks.
4. It was always win-win. "Every time I make someone else feel good, I can't help feeling better myself."

Tell three people you appreciate them — and why

The heading above was actually an assignment I gave to my Psychology students early each year. I can't think of a better way to end this chapter than to give it to my readers. It's simple: think of three people you greatly appreciate. The odds are that you rarely, if ever, tell them. So, the assignment is to tell them and give them the reason. Do this verbally and face-to-face, not via e-mail, text, phone, letter, card, Facebook, or Twitter. See what happens. I guarantee that each time you do it you'll make two people feel really good.

Never underestimate the power of a kind word.

—*Mirela Monte*

Personal Notes

Personal Notes

chapter 14
Two words can change a life

Whether within our own thoughts, spoken or written, words have the power to transform the world we live in.

—*Carisa Rasmussen*

A few reminders about the power of words

This is somewhat of an extension of the previous chapter about the power of words. They can be toxic or nourishing, they can hurt or heal, they can tear down or build up, they can discourage or encourage. They can be life-changing in ways both bad and good. That chapter was essentially about the impact our words have on others. The main reason was to help you increase your awareness of the power of words, and to urge you to choose words that are positive and affirming.

This chapter also deals with words and their impact, but in a completely different way. It isn't about how your words affect other people's lives. And it's not about how other people's words affect your life. It's about how two simple words can dramatically affect your life. If you put them to use, they can get you to think more about the power of self-talk, and they can inspire you to make the most out of every day in your life.

They're two words that you read about way back in Chapter 6. Do you remember the story about my friend in college, Bruce Diaso, who was paralyzed with polio? Do you remember the two words that had taken hold of him, and had soured his thoughts and his life after he got polio? They were *anger* and *self-pity*. His doctor asked him if they were making things better or worse for him. He realized that he was poisoning himself, so he chose two new words to live by:

OPPORTUNITY and THANKFULNESS

I wrote only briefly about each word in Chapter 6 because I'd already planned an entire chapter on them later in the book. These two words changed Bruce's life. He thought about them every day, he repeatedly said them to himself, and he lived by them. These two words also changed my life. As I wrote earlier, my talk with Bruce when I was 19 years old was one of the "defining moments" of my life. I think about these two words every day, I repeatedly say them to myself, and I try to live by them.

Thanks to Bruce, these two words have also changed the lives of hundreds of other people between 1972 and the present. Bruce died in 1972, and that was the year I started sharing with others what this great young man had taught me. I shared it with my high school and college students for almost 30 years, I've written about it in three of my books, and I share it with people of all walks of life in many of my speaking engagements.

I've received hundreds of letters and e-mails that say, "Your two words really did change my life." My response is always the same, "No, Bruce's two words changed your life."

Then I thank them for the positive feedback. A woman real-tor in Florida wrote a beautiful letter to me shortly after I spoke at her company's national conference. My favorite part of it said, "You were so lucky to have Bruce in your life. Thank you for telling us his story, because now he's in my life also. Even though I never met him, and he's been gone for many years, he provided a 'defining moment' for me (through you) as well. My life has had a lot of emotional pain in it the last four years, and those two words were just what I needed to hear. I hope you'll share Bruce's story and his two words with everyone you can."

Let's examine each of the two words a little more fully.

Opportunity

> *Every day is a new opportunity. You can build on yesterday's success or put its failures behind and start over again. That's the way life is, with a new game every day...*
>
> —Bob Feller (1918-2010)
> Hall of Fame baseball pitcher

> *The golden opportunity you are seeking is in yourself. It is not in your environment; it is not in luck or chance, or the help of others; it is in yourself alone.*
>
> —Orison Swett Marden (1850-1924)
> Founder of Success Magazine

The dictionary defines opportunity as "a good chance for advancement or progress." That's what we have facing us when we wake up every morning. Every day presents us with countless opportunities. What kind of opportunities? The kind I've been writing about throughout this book. Here are just a few of them. We have the opportunity every day to. . .

...build character ...practice self-control   ...improve our attitudes

...love someone   ...be honest in all things ...do an act of kindness

...work hard   ...feed our minds   ...care for our bodies

...use kind words ...learn from a mentor   ...be wise with money

In helping my students see their countless opportunities, I also wanted to help them understand the impact of their words on themselves. For instance, I would ask them if going to school was an obligation. The answer was always a resounding YES the first time around. I asked why they looked at school as an obligation. The most frequent answer was, "Because we *have* to go." I asked them if using words other than *obligation* and *have to* would make a difference. This, of course, totally confused them, so they asked what I meant. I was ready. "How about looking upon school as an *opportunity* instead of as an *obligation*? How about saying "I *get* to go to school" instead of saying "I *have* to go to school?" As you can imagine, there were a few groans and a lot of laughs. They thought I was joking, as well as being corny.

But they were open to hearing my explanation, so I used a teacher's most powerful tool—stories. I told them stories about some of the countries I've been to that are mired in poverty, and where education isn't mandatory. I told them I saw 14 year old kids who didn't know how to read or write, were working jobs that required hard physical labor, and were stuck in a dead-end system with no chance of ever improving the quality of their lives.

I said, "Think how fortunate you are. Five days a week you have an opportunity to come to a place where you'll be with your friends, where you'll be with dedicated teachers who care about you and help you learn. Most important, you have the opportunity to come to a place every day in which you can work toward achieving something with your life." I also reminded them that they live in a country often called "the land of opportunity." By this time they understood that I wasn't joking. And after a lengthy discussion, they admitted that they often take school for granted, and that it would be helpful to look at it in another way.

The truth is, the words we use to describe anything are a reflection of our attitudes toward it. Some people see problems, failures, disappointments, roadblocks, difficulties, misfortunes, defeats, and obligations. Others see opportunities in each one of them. As Bruce said, "Every day is full of opportunities. It's too bad more people don't see them."

Thankfulness

The happiest people in the world aren't the ones who have everything. The happiest people are the ones who appreciate what they do have.

—Ruth Urban

In Chapter 17 I write about real heroes. It includes a story about my mom and the twelve words that best described her. If I had to pick just one of them, it would be *thankful*. Thankfulness was her cornerstone and her foundation. She appreciated life and everything in it, especially her family. And she never missed an opportunity to say "thank you," whether it was face-to-face, over the phone, or through one of the thousands (literally) of hand written notes she sent to people throughout her life.

On the day that Bruce Diaso told me that *thankfulness* was one of the keys to his life, I said, "You remind me of my mom. She constantly reminds me to be thankful for what I have." Bruce replied, "Your mom is a wise woman." He asked me *how* she taught me to be thankful. I remember then, as I do today, two specific things she did to teach me to live every day with a heart full of appreciation.

The first one was when I was about 11, and was whining about something the other kids had, but I didn't. Now, please read the quote at the top of this page again. That's what she said to me in her sweet and gentle voice. I heard her say it often. Like a good teacher, she reinforced it regularly, and I've never forgotten it.

The other thing she did was use pictures. There's an old saying that "a picture is worth a thousand words." My mom knew it well. We subscribed to *LIFE* magazine, and it often had large pictures of people, especially children, in other parts of the world. It seemed like every issue reminded me how much poverty there was in the world. My mom opened that magazine to those pictures every time I complained about how rough my life was. And again in her sweet and gentle way, she said, "Count your blessings." Those pictures left a deep impression on me, and reminded me often how fortunate I was. Sadly, the world has more poverty and illness in it today than it did back in the 1950s, and I can see even more depressing pictures in magazines, newspapers, on TV news, and on the Internet. If we have a place to live, food to eat, clothes to wear, an education, and money to spend on the other things we need, we have it better than literally billions of people.

Here are some reminders about how good we have it:

- Eighty percent of the people in the world live in substandard housing

- Eighty percent live on less than ten dollars a day

- Fifty percent are undernourished, many of them starving

- Thirty-three percent have no access to safe water

- Twenty-four percent have no electricity

- Sixty-seven percent can't read or write

- Seven percent have access to the Internet

- One percent of them have a college education

We have it pretty good, don't we? The key is being thankful. It's a way of looking at life, it's an attitude, and it can become a habit—the best one you'll ever have. See the opportunities life offers you and be thankful for them.

> *If you concentrate on finding whatever is good in every situation, you will discover that your life will suddenly be filled with gratitude, a feeling that nurtures the soul.*
>
> —*Rabbi Harold Kushner*

> *To speak gratitude is courteous and pleasant, to enact gratitude is generous and noble, but to live gratitude is to touch Heaven.*
>
> —*Johannes A. Gaertner*

Personal Notes

Personal Notes

chapter 15 *You're more likely to succeed if you have good mentors*

Good mentors offer priceless advice that comes from their own experiences—both successes and failures. They teach us, they guide us, they encourage us, and they increase our chances for success in life. Every kid and every adult should have mentors.

—Lorraine G. Kirk, Ph.D.

Defining mentor

Whether you know what a mentor is probably depends on your age. Most kids haven't heard the term. Most adults have. But there are different types of mentors, so this chapter also begins with a definition:

A mentor is an experienced adviser and supporter

There are different types of mentors:

Corporate mentor—an experienced person who works for a company, and is assigned to mentor someone recently hired.

Professional mentor—a person someone hires to help him develop skills in a particular field.

Life coach—also a person someone hires, but to help her function better in various aspects of life.

Each of these types of mentors can be valuable, depending on a person's needs at a particular stage in his life. But none of these is the type of mentor discussed here. The next type is the focus of this chapter.

Personal mentor—someone who is older and wiser, who is always there for you, who cares about you, who teaches you, and who helps you become a better person. Personal mentors do not charge anything. They mentor because they find great joy in helping another person understand and deal with life more effectively.

The rewards of having a mentor

A mentor is someone who sees the potential within you better than you see it yourself. A mentor brings out the best in you.

—Joel P. Humphries

Here's a list of some of the rewards and benefits of having a mentor:

- **Knowledge**—Because mentors have lived longer, they've learned more, and they know more than we do, especially in the areas of their expertise. A good mentor is a good teacher. Example: A few people have told you that you need to improve your social skills (we all need to improve them). You have a mentor who has excellent social skills such as listening, making eye contact, smiling, speaking clearly, and using effective body language. It took years to develop these skills, so your mentor passes on to you both what and how he learned.

- **Experience**—Mentors, because they've been involved in a field for several years, have developed understanding and skills in particular areas. Example: You want to write a book and get it published. It's much more complex and difficult than most people realize. A published author can give you valuable tips throughout the entire process.

- **Wisdom**—This a combination of knowledge and experience. It's a deep understanding of how life works. Example: You're down in the dumps because you didn't get accepted into the college that was your first choice. Your mentor can explain to you that this happens to more than a million students per year. You need to have a Plan B. And you just might be better off by attending one of the other colleges on your list.

- **Encouragement**—This word literally means "to give courage." It's a strong need everyone has during various stages in life. Mentors are wonderful at encouragement. They give us that little positive push in the right direction just when we need it. Example: A young person is afraid to enter a speaking contest for fear of failing. The mentor would point out that everyone fails from time to time, and would explain some of his own failures. The biggest failure is in not trying.

- **Friendship**—There are few things in life more joyful than friendship (see Chapter 18). A mentor may or may not start as a friend, but I can assure you that she will be after advising and helping you, no matter what the area is. The simple truth is that we like and admire people who help us. Example: I once thought it was impossible to forgive certain acts, especially cruel ones. But a mentor convinced me otherwise, and he taught me the freedom of forgiveness. I grew to respect that man for his wisdom and to love him for his kindness.

- **Comfort**—Mentors not only help us develop a variety of skills and increase our knowledge, they seem to always be there when we need them, especially in hard times. Example: Let's say someone you love and trust betrays you. It hurts deeply. This is often when mentors are at their most valuable. They've been through and survived these kinds of painful experiences. They can help us understand that we're not alone, and they can help us deal with the hurt.

> *The value of a good mentor is immeasurable.*
> *—Christian Beauford*

Where do mentors come from?

> *When the student is ready, the teacher will appear.*
> *—Buddha*

The answer to the above question is simple: they just seem to show up when we need them. However, it may take a little effort on our part. Sometimes we need to ask around a bit. At other times someone will know our needs at a particular time, and recommend a mentor. And at other times we already know whom to ask. Believe me, they're out there and they're willing to help us. It's actually one of the primary purposes of life: to pass on what we've learned to the next generation. Sometimes even to our own generation.

Who are they? They're anyone who's experienced, has knowledge, is caring, and is wise. Are parents mentors? In most cases, no. Good parents teach their children valuable things, often for a lifetime. But in most cases, mentors come from outside the home. Are grandparents mentors? Absolutely, and sometimes they're the best ones. They usually don't live with you, yet they love and care about you. They want the best for you, and they're always willing to help you in any way they can.

Most mentors come from outside our families. Even though we don't always notice them, they're around us all the time. As Buddha says above, when the student is ready, the teacher appears. When we need to learn something or improve ourselves, there's always a mentor available. It might be someone who's been in your life for a long time, and you suddenly realize something valuable: This person can help me.

Listen to advice and accept instruction,
and in the end you will be wise.

—*King Solomon, Proverbs 19:20*

The rewards of being a mentor

It's important to understand that a person can have mentors and be a mentor at the same time. It all depends on one's age, needs, and experiences. I'm always reminded of my youngest mentor when I speak or write about this subject. I was 46 when I got my first computer. It was a Mac SE, something you might see in a museum today. One of my friends had one, showed it to me, and enthusiastically convinced me that I also had to have one. So, just as I'm getting adjusted to my electric typewriter (another museum piece), something new comes along. Wanting to keep up, I bought my first Mac. But it sat there on my desk for about three weeks. I was terrified of it. I didn't know how to hook it up or how to use it, and I'm not good at reading instructions, especially when they're in another language. I call the language "computer-speak." There were just too many terms I didn't understand. To this day, I have no idea what a gigabyte is.

After a few weeks I decided that to let this little machine intimidate me like this was silly. It was also a waste of hard-earned money if I didn't use it. So I started asking around. One of the secretaries at school told me her son was a whiz at computers, and that he would be happy to help me get started. I accepted the offer and we agreed on a time that he would come to my home the next day. The doorbell rang, I opened the door, and didn't see anyone or a car. Then I looked down and saw Chris. He was about four feet tall (I'm six-foot-five), was 11 years old, and had ridden his bicycle to my house. But he knew a lot more than I did about computers. He had me hooked up and typing away in no time. Chris probably didn't know what a mentor was, but he was a good one that day. When he left, I thanked him, and gave him a little reward. He said, "It was really fun teaching a teacher something he didn't know."

In a very real way, little 11 year old Chris captured the essence of what it means to be a mentor, and what the reward is. It *is* fun helping someone else. In addition to fun, we might add gratifying, fulfilling, and meaningful. It feels good to help another person. This was one of the main points made in Chapter 8, which is about kindness.

Mentoring is always win-win. The mentor is rewarded in at least one way the person being mentored is: friendship. It's a natural consequence of one person helping another. But the other rewards are different. They center on the satisfaction of knowing that we contributed something positive to the life of another person. This is the way we're wired. This is why we're here. I want to close by repeating part of a quotation I used at the beginning of this book:

> ... *Having an impact on another person, shaping his life in some small but vital way, is one of the most enduring satisfactions we will know.*
>
> —*Rabbi Harold Kushner*

PERSONAL NOTES

Personal Notes

chapter 16
Popular culture and technology are powerful—in ways both good and bad

Americans spend two-thirds of our waking lives consuming mass media. Be it television, movies, music, video games, or the internet, media consumption is the number one activity of choice for Americans—commanding, on average, 3700 hours of each citizen's time annually.

—Karen E. Dill, Ph.D.
Professor of psychology

Culture, pop culture, and technology

As previously stated, it helps a reader to know the meaning an author is attaching to a key word. It's why several chapters in this book begin with a definition. This one has three.

Culture –In the broadest sense it means "the way we live." It includes our history, values, system of government, economic system (how we distribute wealth), belief systems (faiths), style (clothing and grooming), language, food, geography, and forms of entertainment. In other words, our culture includes everything that has an effect on our daily lives. Cultural anthropologists frequently use the term *enculturation*. It means that as we grow and develop, our culture plays a large part in shaping us, even though we may not be aware of it. Imagine how differently you would live and think and talk if you were born and raised in China, Nigeria, or Morocco.

Popular culture (also called pop culture)—This is an aspect of our main culture which represents what's currently popular, or as some people say, "what's trending now." The centerpiece of popular culture is the entertainment industry. This includes movies, TV, music, sports, video games, social networks, fashion, and celebrities (discussed in the next chapter). Pop culture has enormous influence on both kids and adults, primarily for these reasons:

- People of all ages love to be entertained.

- We now have more choices as to *how* we want to be entertained.

- Modern technology, particularly the Internet, has made it easier to access these forms of entertainment.

- When something happens in the entertainment industry we learn about it almost instantaneously.

- The influence of pop culture is so pervasive that it would be almost impossible to not be affected by it.

- A high percentage of American people love glitz, glamour, wealth, gossip, and sensationalism. The media, understanding this, feeds us a steady diet of all of them.

The purpose of listing these spheres of influence is to neither condemn nor criticize popular culture or the people of our country. For the most part, they're statements of fact. I just want to remind my readers that this is the world we live in. Popular culture is a powerful force. Whether that powerful force is good for us or bad for us is determined by the choices we make. Remember the title of Chapter 10? "You are who you are because of what goes into your mind."

Technology—In the broadest sense it's defined as the application of scientific knowledge for practical purposes. We use technology to open our garage doors, design buildings, detect illnesses, check out at the grocery store, find an address while in a car, and to do countless other things that make life easier and more efficient for us on a day-to-day basis.

Technology in this chapter refers more specifically to the electronic "toys" we use to be part of popular culture. It includes desktop and laptop computers, the Internet, smart phones, TV's, electronic tablets, digital photography, video games, MP3 players, and social networks on the web.

How we spend our time—a few statistics

Time is life. It is irreversible and irreplaceable. To waste your time is to waste your life, but to master your time is to master your life and make the most of it.

—Alan Lakein
Time efficiency expert

Several individuals and organizations have conducted research in recent years to answer two questions about the American public (especially youth) and the entertainment media: 1. How much time is spent being "wired" (connected to the media)? 2. What are the effects? Dr. Karen Dill, a psychology professor quoted at the beginning of this chapter, says we spend two-thirds of the time we're awake consuming popular culture with our electronic tools. Here are some related statistics, most of them from a major study conducted in 2011 by the Kaiser Family Foundation.

- In 1995 kids between the ages of 8-18 spent 28 hours per week, or 4 hours per day, connected to the media.

- In 2011 kids in that same age group spent 53 hours per week, or 7.5 hours per day, connected to the media.

- Seventy percent of the kids surveyed said there were no rules in their home governing time spent in mass media consumption.

- More than two-thirds of our 8-18 year olds have cell phones and MP3s.

- Students in grades 7-12 spend more than an hour and a half each day sending text messages, or about 118 messages per day. Some adults do the same.

- A little more than 92 percent of kids 8-18 play video games. About 8.5 percent have been determined addicted. This means that their video game playing interferes with other aspects of their lives.

- The average American adult spends 8.5 hours per day (including work) looking at a screen—computer, Internet, mobile phone, video, social network, GPS, or TV. The latter is their top choice. According to the Nielsen Company, the average adult spends 5 hours a day watching TV—61 minutes watching ads.

The best and the worst

I don't report the above statistics because I think they represent the downfall of our country. I report them because precise numbers based on solid research give us a more accurate picture of what's going on. Psychologists and sociologists agree that these findings have elements of both good and bad in them. Here are some of the main ones:

The best of popular culture and technology:

1. Millions of people of all ages have become tech-savvy (how I wish I was one of them). The electronic devices we have access to today are nothing short of phenomenal, and new ones keep coming. Properly used, they can help us learn, stay connected, be informed, and do a number of tasks more quickly and efficiently.

2. We not only love to be entertained, we *need* to be entertained. It gives us a break from our responsibilities and some of the hardships of life. Today's technology and popular culture fill this need by offering us some dazzling and spectacular choices.

3. We're better connected with each other and with the world around us than we've ever been.

4. We can learn more quickly and can be better informed than any generation before us.

5. Students at all grade levels, if they're taught to use their time and their electronic tools wisely, can dramatically improve their grades.

6. GIGO—Good In, Good Out. Remember that you are what you are because of what goes into your mind. The Internet

and the entertainment industry offer plenty of good choices. It's up to you to make them.

The worst of popular culture and technology:

1. There are more predators out there than we'll ever know. They come in different varieties. The worst ones are sexual molesters who hack into e-mail addresses and become "friends" on our social networks. Next in line are the predators who want our identities and our money. Everyone needs to be aware of these people and learn how to protect ourselves against them.

2. Spending too much time connected to the media can ultimately become anti-social. Even if we're making contact on Facebook or Twitter or sending text messages for hours a day, we're not having face-to-face contact with other people. It's one of our greatest needs. Our friends are better in person, and they help us develop the social skills we need.

3. We now know that a number of aspects of the entertainment world and the technology that goes with them can be highly addictive. A few of them are video games, texting, TV, pornography, buying things on the Internet, and social networks. Of these, I oppose only pornography (more on this later), but too much time with any of them can lead to serious problems. As stated earlier, addictions interfere with other aspects of our lives—the things we should be devoting more of our time to.

4. Another drawback of too much media time has to do with the damage it does to a person's attention span. People who spend several hours per day using our incredibly quick and entertaining electronic toys (often more than one at a time) find it increasingly difficult to stay properly focused on other matters that require longer periods of attention. Examples

are attending school, working, playing sports, reading, writing, and even socializing in person.

5. Students without any monitoring, without any rules, and without good advice about moderation in all things pertaining to the mass media, perform poorly in school.

6. GIGO—Garbage In, Garbage Out. Remember that you are what you are because of what goes into your mind. The Internet and the entertainment industry offer plenty of choices, both good and bad. The rest is up to you.

Four danger zones that are part of popular culture

In the introduction I wrote about the desire to make this a positive and upbeat book. But as explained in Chapter 4, I also want to be realistic. That chapter is about the pain and suffering we all experience because they're part of life. The positive comes when we learn how to deal with them and how to grow from them. This part of Chapter 16 is similar in that it discusses four other realities that have become part of everyday life. We also have to learn the most effective ways to deal with them.

Each one can tempt us, each one has the potential to cause great harm, and each one is a test of our character. In a book of this nature and size these topics can't be covered in great detail, but because they're all a big part of popular culture, they need to be addressed. The first two are glamorized in the media and by peers. The next two are glamorized mostly by peers.

1. Sex—For about the first 350 years of our history, sex was a private matter. That changed in the late 1960s. And since then we've been increasingly bombarded with messages about sex, sex, and more sex. As stated on the Great Schools website (greatschools.org), "Sex is everywhere." It's glorified in advertising, music, videos, TV shows, magazines, books, movies, and most blatantly in the online pornography industry. In the process something beautiful has been made dirty and sleazy, or simply recreational. Extensive research tells us that this cheapening of sex is causing serious problems for millions of children, teenagers, and adults.

Here are some of those problems caused by what a friend of mine calls "our hyper-sexualized popular culture": promiscuity, sexual addictions, infidelity, unwed pregnancies, abortions, fatherless children, sexually transmitted diseases, and damage done to marriages and families. Again, we reap what we sow. Poor sexual choices can often result in devastating life consequences.

Maybe you're wondering if I have a solution to these problems that come from the "sexploitation" of America. While I can't make it go away any more than I can make pain and suffering go away, I *can* offer a few suggestions for dealing with it.

In the case of children and teenagers, parents need to take responsibility in this critically important area. In a perfect world parents would diligently screen viewing material and lovingly teach and advise their children about the dangers and consequences associated with the continual escalation of sexual messages. Unfortunately, we know from research that not nearly enough parents do this. Too many avoid the issue, thereby compounding the problem. And when they avoid it, kids take on the attitude toward sex that's glorified in the media and talked up by their peers. I would advise parents to begin by reading the Kaiser Family Foundation 2007 report called "Parents, Children & Media." Google makes it easy to find on the Internet.

I would also suggest that parents who feel uncomfortable or inadequate in addressing the problem seek help from people, books, and websites devoted to the field. There are helpful books, such as *How to Talk to Your Child about Sex* by Linda and Richard Eyre, and *Everything You Never Wanted Your Kids to Know About Sex (But Were Afraid They'd Ask): The Secrets to Surviving Your Child's Sexual Development from Birth to the Teens* by Dr. Justin Richardson and Dr. Mark Schuster. There are also several helpful websites. Two of them are goodhousekeeping.com/family/tweens and birdsandbeesandkids.com.

In the case of adults, the number one problem is addiction, particularly to online pornography. An expert told Oprah Winfrey on her show in 2007 that porn on the Internet is the "crack cocaine" of sexual addiction. Here are a few statistics that support his statement: twelve percent of all websites are pornographic, which means there are close to 25 million such sites; 40 million Americans are regular visitors to online porn; 20 percent of men admit to watching porn online at work. The possible results? The end of marriages and other relationships, poor performance in school, loss of jobs, and feelings of shame.

Again, help is available in a variety of forms: professional counselors, mentors, organizations, leaders in faith communities, books, websites, friends, relatives, and people who have conquered the problem. The most important step is the first one: admitting to someone that you have the problem. The second step, almost as important, is being held accountable to one or more people on a regular basis. Sexual addiction can be cured. There are countless success stories that prove this point. If you have a problem, take that all-important first step.

2. Alcohol—This is one of those issues in which both kids and adults get a double-whammy. Drinking (including drunkenness) is glorified and advertised in the media, and there's enormous peer pressure to drink and be cool. Please understand that I'm not suggesting that we rid our country of all alcohol. We tried that once (it was called Prohibition), and it only made matters worse. The key word here is *responsibility*. It's the responsibility of people under the age of 21 to respect the law, and it's the responsibility of those over 21 to either not drink or to drink responsibly.

Here are a few statistics from Learn-About-Alcoholism. com:

- Alcohol is the number one drug in America.

- There are more than 12 million alcoholics in the U.S.

- Three-fourths of all adults drink alcohol, and 6 percent of them are alcoholics.

- Americans spend $197 million each day on alcohol.

- In the U.S. a person is killed in an alcohol-related car accident every 30 seconds.

- A 2000 study found that nearly 7 million persons ages 12-20 were binge drinkers.

- Three-fourths of all high school seniors report being drunk at least once.

- Adolescents who begin drinking before the age of 15 are four times more likely to become alcoholics than their counterparts who don't begin drinking until the age of 21.

How does a young person of good character handle the alcohol issue? By developing self-control (the master skill of life) and having the courage to say "no" despite peer pressure. Also by showing respect for his family and for the law. An adult with good character also practices self-control in knowing when to not drink, and if she does, to drink in a responsible manner.

3. Drugs—How would you respond if I asked you to poison yourself? I'm guessing your answer would be either, "No way!" or "Get out of here." But the sad truth is that millions of people, both kids and adults, are poisoning themselves with illegal drugs on a daily basis. And in doing so they risk destroying their lives. The media often makes using marijuana and cocaine look as if it's a routine activity. Fortunately, it doesn't glamorize other deadly drugs. But peers do. "C'mon, let's get high. It's a blast."

Here's a frightening statistic found in the 2010 "National Survey on Drug Use and Health" by the U.S. Substance Abuse and Mental Health Services Administration: "8.7 percent of the population 12 years and older use illicit drugs including marijuana, cocaine (including crack), heroin, hallucinogens, inhalants, or prescription drugs used non-medically." In other words, people are, in fact, choosing to poison themselves. Why? Either because of peer pressure to be cool or the inability to deal with the realities of life.

I don't think my suggestions here will surprise anyone. I'll put them in the form of three questions: 1. Do you want to be a weak person who does drugs only because others are doing it? 2. Do you want to poison and destroy yourself? 3. What goes into your body? Is it toxic or nourishing?

4. Tobacco—Until the early 1970s smoking cigarettes was glamorized in the media almost as much as sex and alcohol were. People smoked in the movies, on TV, and in public life. Cigarettes were advertised widely on TV, on the radio, and in magazines and newspapers. Celebrities, including famous athletes, made commercials showing just how sophisticated and cool it was to smoke. But all of that changed after we learned how deadly smoking can be. Both the federal and state governments have clamped down on advertising cigarettes and have invoked strict laws as to where people can and cannot smoke. They've also levied high taxes on cigarettes as part of a national campaign to discourage people from smoking and damaging their health.

While all of this has gotten millions of people to give up this nasty habit and has convinced millions more to not take it up, people continue to smoke and shorten their lives. Here are some scary statistics provided by Smoking-Facts.Net:

- More than 43 million people in the U.S. smoke regularly.

- Each day 3000 children smoke their first cigarette. One third of them will eventually die from smoking.

- At least 90 percent of adult smokers started when they were teenagers, and then got "hooked." They all started because their friends smoked, it looked adult, and it was cool.

- More than 20 percent (6 million) of today's teenagers smoke even though they know it is addictive and leads to disease.

- Kids who smoke cigarettes are 3 times more likely to drink alcohol, 8 times more likely to smoke marijuana, and 22 times more likely to use cocaine and other drugs.

My advice here is the same as it is for using drugs (tobacco is an addictive drug). Three questions: 1. Do you want to be a weak person who smokes only because others are doing it? 2. Do you want to poison and destroy yourself? 3. What goes into your body? Is it toxic or nourishing?

A few reminders

I want to close this chapter about the influence of popular culture by reinforcing a few points made earlier:

- Popular culture is one of the most powerful forces in our society. We're all affected by it in one way or another.

- It has the potential to have either a positive or a negative influence on our lives.

- We are what we are because of what goes into our minds.

- We choose what goes into our minds.

The world we live in has a mixture of things that can be good for us and things that can be bad for us. We're choosing between them every minute that we're awake. We are the sum total of our choices.

—Margery Nyman

Personal Notes

Personal Notes

chapter 17 We should be inspired by real heroes, not celebrities

> *When it comes to knowing the difference between a hero and a celebrity, our society is confused. Massively, profoundly confused.*
>
> —*T.A. Barron*
> *Family Circle Magazine*

Who are your heroes?

I've been asking the above question to both kids and adults for more than 40 years. I've asked it under many different circumstances. For instance, while teaching in high school, I would give my students a small piece of paper and ask them to write the names of their top three heroes on it. I would do the same thing with my adult college students, who were mostly in the 30-45 age group.

I left the classroom in 2001, but (as of this writing) continue to speak to teachers, students of all ages, and parents throughout the country. When time allows, I do the same exercise with these groups. When there's less time, I ask all the people in the audience to think of their number one hero. I then call on about five or six people and ask for their hero's name. Their responses are the beginning of my presentation. The answers I've received over the years have fallen into one of four categories:

1. Celebrities—those who are famous because they're movie and/or TV stars, great athletes, popular musicians, or extremely wealthy.

2. World or national leaders—those who have brought about change as a result of their sacrifice, courage, and hard work. Examples are Martin Luther King, Jr., Mother Teresa, Nelson Mandela, Anne Frank, Albert Schweitzer, Harriet Tubman, Rosa Parks, George Washington, and Abraham Lincoln.

3. People who risk their lives for others—those in the military, police officers, and fire department workers.

4. Personal heroes—those who are, or have been, part of our personal lives. They serve as wonderful role models who consistently demonstrate outstanding character traits, influence us in positive ways, and inspire us and others to be at our best.

Which type of answers did I receive most frequently? Among students ages 8-18, celebrities were named more than 90 percent of the time. Among adults of all ages only 11 percent named celebrities. The rest of them named world or national leaders (22 percent) and personal role models (67 percent). What person pops into your mind when I ask, "Who is your number one hero?" Is it a celebrity or a real hero?

This chapter is about only two of the above four categories: celebrities and personal heroes. I have enormous respect and admiration for great world and national leaders of both past and present, and I'm deeply grateful for the courageous people who serve in the military, do police work, and perform many critical tasks in fire departments. Virtually everyone admires these people, and there's no confusion about them or their value to society. But there *is* great confusion about the importance and value of celebrities, and the difference between them and real heroes.

"Massively, profoundly confused"

The quotation by T. A. Barron in *Family Circle Magazine* at the beginning of this chapter is the best possible introduction for this topic. We do, indeed, seem to be massively, profoundly confused about the difference between a celebrity and a real hero. Mr. Barron goes on to address this confusion. He writes, "While celebrity just means fame—someone whose name, face, or singing voice is widely recognized—heroism means something more. Something that represents the best of who we are as a people." He continues, "For starters, a hero is not about fame. Or money. Or Grammy awards. A hero is about just one thing, and that's *character*. That's right—qualities such a courage, compassion, hope, perseverance, humility, and faith. Qualities with deep value and lasting importance." Thank you, Mr. Barron, for describing our real heroes so eloquently. Remember the title of Chapter 1? "Good character is the foundation of a good life."

A clarification: this chapter is in no way an attack or condemnation of celebrities. They play a vital role in our society. For the most part they're great looking, extremely talented, and highly entertaining. They provide us with a wonderful escape from some of the rigors of daily life. A high percentage of people greatly enjoy movies, TV, sports, and music. I'm one of them, and am thankful that we have these gifted people in our culture.

But do we really need to know everything about their private lives? Do we need to know who put on or lost 20 pounds? Do we need to know who wore what to where? Do we need to know who's dating whom and who's cheating on whom? Do we need to see pictures of their babies, their mansions, their jewelry, their exotic car collections? Do we need to know where they were spotted recently? Do we need to watch all the TV programs devoted to the latest gossip about them? Do we need to read all the magazines and tabloids that cover their private lives, often stretching the truth? Do we need to buy products that are endorsed by celebrities? Will having them make us more cool? But most important, do we need to put them on pedestals and worship them?

Real heroes

A personal hero is someone who makes you want to be a better person by showing you how.

—Christopher L. Grey

One of the definitions of *hero* is "a person who is admired." That's pretty broad, so it could include celebrities, great leaders of the past and present, and those who serve their country or their community. We admire a lot of people for a lot of different reasons.

But this chapter is about a different type of hero—one who is in our personal circle of family and friends, one who touches our lives in the best way possible. Here are some examples of whom they might be: parent, grandparent, brother or sister, extended family member, teacher, classmate, coach, teammate, priest, minister, rabbi, other religious leader, friend, co-worker, professional colleague. These people are all around us, and a select few of them become our heroes. We respect and admire them so much that they inspire us to be like them.

Earlier in this chapter Mr. Barron said, "A hero is about just one thing, and that's *character.*" Good character is what this book is all about. The best examples of it are in our midst. They teach what it is, not by telling us, but by living it. In the Character Education movement we often refer to the three aspects of good character that these real heroes understand:

1. **Know the good**
2. **Love the good**
3. **Do the good**

A quiz about celebrities and heroes

While I was writing this chapter, a friend sent me one of those e-mails that goes viral over the Internet. The subject line said "Charles Schulz' Philosophy Of Life," and there was a little quiz attached. In case you're not aware, Schulz (1922-2000) was the creator of one of the most popular cartoon strips of all time—"Peanuts." The quiz is attributed to him, but there's no evidence that it he wrote it. Whether it was written by Schulz or someone else, it's a wonderful reminder about the people in our lives who really do matter.

1. *Name the five wealthiest people in the world.*

2. *Name the last five Heisman trophy winners.*

3. *Name the last five winners of the Miss America contest.*

4. *Name ten people who have won the Nobel or Pulitzer Prize.*

5. *Name the last half dozen Academy Award winners for best actor and actress.*

6. *Name the last decade's worth of World Series winners.*

How did you do? The point is, none of us remember the headliners of yesterday. These are no second-rate achievers. They are the best in their fields. But the applause dies. Awards tarnish. Achievements are forgotten. Accolades and certificates are buried with their owners.

Here's another quiz. See how you do on this one:

1. *List a few teachers who aided your journey through school.*

2. *Name three friends who have helped you through a difficult time.*

3. *Name five people who have taught you something worthwhile.*

4. *Think of a few people who have made you feel appreciated and special.*

5. *Think of five people you enjoy spending time with.*

6. *Name half a dozen heroes whose stories have inspired you.*

Easier?

The lesson: The people who make a difference in your life are not the ones with the most credentials, the most money, or the most awards. They are the ones that care.

> *Fame is a vapor, popularity an accident, riches take wing, and only character endures.*
>
> —Horace Greeley

The author's number one hero

I want to close this chapter on a personal note, and at the same time give my readers an excellent example of a personal hero. While I've had, and still have, many personal heroes, my mom, Ruth Urban (1913-2009), is far and away my number one. The best way to describe her is to borrow from one of the four pages in her memorial service program. While putting it together before printing, we decided to have one page that contained only the words that best described her.

I asked family members and other people who knew her, "What words come to your mind first when you hear the name Ruth Urban?" These are the ones that came up over and over:

Humble	Patient	Kind
Honest	Considerate	Forgiving
Caring	Loving	Giving
Thankful	Generous	Courageous

These twelve words describe a person of good character. They describe a person who qualifies as a genuine personal hero. As wonderful as my mom was, there are other people around us who have some or all of these same qualities. And the best news of all is that you have some people like this in your own life. Make them your heroes. Make them your role models. Learn from them. Be like them.

A hero is someone who makes a difference in
your life, someone who brings out the best in you,
someone who inspires you to do the same for others.

—*Dana Lavinsky*

PERSONAL NOTES

PERSONAL NOTES

chapter

18 *Nothing is more precious than friendship*

Life is to be fortified by many friendships. To love, and be loved, is the greatest happiness of existence.

—*Sydney Smith*

Defining real friendship

Two of the most difficult words to define are *love* and *friendship*. And they just happen to be closely related. Back in Chapter 5, I used two key words to define love: *kindness* and *giving*. These are also the main ingredients of true friendship. Real friends are genuinely kind to each other. And they give each other the best they have.

Sadly, we often take our friends for granted, even though they're often the greatest sources of happiness we'll ever experience. I received a powerful reminder about this in an unexpected place—Egypt—back in 2006. Needing help to get to the most famous places in this ancient and fascinating country, my wife Cathy and I joined ten other people on a tour. Our guide was one of the most interesting, knowledgeable, energetic, and befriended person we had ever met. Among other things, he gave me the title of this chapter.

His name is Moufid Mansour. He had been a dentist who led tours as a hobby because he was so passionate about teaching the history of his country to others. Eventually, his passion overtook him, he closed his dentistry practice, and became a full-time tour guide. He was much in demand. One of the things we noticed about him early on the tour was how many friends he had. Everywhere we went, people went out of their way to greet him with sincere warmth and a big hug. They were genuinely excited to see him. We got the impression that everyone in Egypt knew and loved Moufid.

After about three days of witnessing all of this affection, I said to him, "Moufid, you have so many friends!" Without hesitating for a second, he said something I'll never forget: "Nothing is more precious than friendship." I've never taken my friends for granted, but Moufid reminded me that they *are* truly precious. We were on a coffee break at the time, so the conversation about the importance of friendship continued. We agreed that life would be empty and painful without good friends. And that it's full and joyful *with* them.

A real friend is someone who . . .

. . . you respect and admire

. . . is authentic and always honest with you

. . . you think of first when you want to do something fun

. . . is comforting and supportive during hard times

. . . shares your joy during good times

. . . can always be counted on and trusted

. . . makes you feel important

. . . brings out the best in you

What is a friend? A single soul dwelling in two bodies.

—Aristotle

We become like our friends

*The people we hang out with have a tendency to
rub off on us. We become like the people we spend
the most time with, for good or for bad.*

—*Christopher Farley*

How we're influenced by others, particularly our closest friends, has been well researched and documented. Many have come to the conclusion that we end up as the composite of the five people we spend the most time with. Not everyone agrees with that specific number, but everyone *does* agree that we become like the people we spend the most time with. Here are some of the principal ways in which our friends influence us:

- Attitude—how we think about life

- Values—what becomes important to us

- Respect—how we treat others

- Language—the words we use

- Work ethic—the effort we put into meeting responsibilities

- Money—how we handle it and what we buy

- Leisure time—what we do with it

Examples of negative influence—Because *Life's Greatest Lessons* has been in the prison library system for many years, I've received hundreds of letters from people who are incarcerated. Almost all of them tell me their life stories in great detail. The letters are touching, sad, and all have essentially the same message. These people grew up in dysfunctional homes, and then, as they express it, "got in with the wrong crowd." This led to lives of crime—alcohol, drugs, assault, theft, robbery, and in a few cases, murder.

Examples of positive influence—During the many years that I taught Psychology, I asked my students (seniors in high school) to write down the five people who had the most influence on their lives thus far. I should point out that these students weren't a cross-section of our entire student population. Psychology was an elective course, so they were there by choice. And almost all of them were great kids. Their answers about the five most influential people were no surprise. The ones they mentioned most frequently were parents, grandparents, older brothers and sisters, friends, teachers, coaches, and leaders in their faith. Basically, they "got in with the right crowd." And they were headed in the right direction.

I don't mean to imply that your success or failure in life will be determined solely by your friends. You have the responsibility to make the right choices. But I guarantee that the people you spend the most time with will have a big influence. We know this from both research and from our own experiences: we become like our friends.

Whoever walks with the wise becomes wise,
but the companion of fools will suffer harm.

—Proverbs 13:20

Making new friends—one of the great joys of life

Strangers are just friends I haven't met yet.

—Will Rogers

Some people are very fortunate to have what we call lifetime friends. They either grow up in the same neighborhood or meet in elementary school, and remain inseparable for the rest of their lives. This is truly one of life's greatest blessings. Because I moved away from my home town at age seventeen, and never moved back, I lost contact many years ago with my earliest friends.

Fortunately, those losses were quickly made up for while I was in college. I was in a fraternity in which we took the term "brotherhood" seriously. We were close friends back in the late 1950s and early 1960s, and now more than 50 years later, we're closer than ever. Even though these friends don't go back to my early childhood, they're among the greatest treasures of my life. Few things are more enriching than old friends.

Almost as good as old friends are new friends. They can enrich our lives beyond anything you might imagine. So I want to make a special point of advising you to always be open to this possibility. I was interviewed a few years ago on the radio about my post-teaching career of speaking and writing. The host asked me, "What do you find most rewarding about what you do?" I said, "Having a positive influence on the lives of other people is about as rewarding as it gets. But making new friends is a close second."

I'm not talking about people I met one time, enjoyed their company, then went on my way, never to see or talk to them again. I'm talking about people who touched my life in a special way, ones who I see and have contact with frequently. There are many of them, and I regard them as treasures, just as I do my college friends. They enrich my life. They add joy and meaning to it.

The most exciting thing about this is knowing that there are literally millions of wonderful people out there in your future, no matter what your age. You won't become friends with all of them, but if you're open to it, you *will* become friends with a surprising number of them. And you'll discover, as I did, that this is one of the most positive, exciting, and rewarding things that can ever happen to you.

You don't have to be a traveling speaker to meet new people and make new friends. You just have to look around.

You're surrounded almost every day by people who just might touch your life in a positive and lasting way. Here are a few examples of places in which I've formed dear friendships in recent years: my place of worship, recreational sports, classes I've attended, the gym in which I work out, and places where I do business. Your places will be different, but those future friends are out there.

> *Make new friends and keep the old.*
> *One is silver, the other is gold.*
>
> —*Girl Scout Song*

Are social network "friends" real friends?

The question above is in no way a criticism of social networks. They're a big part of our culture and they're immensely popular with millions of people of all ages from all over the world. There's plenty of evidence that social networks have been a powerful force for good in many ways. A study conducted in 2011 tells us that American Internet users spend 16 percent of their time online on social networking sites. The primary reason is that it helps people stay informed and connected.

But like everything else, social networks have their drawbacks. Here are a few: many employees are on social networks when they're supposed to be working, people of all ages can get addicted to them, students who spend too much time on them do poorly in school, many people portray themselves as something they're not, and "friends" on a social network often cheapen the meaning of a real friend. Someone recently asked me if I would be a "friend" on her Facebook page. I hardly knew her, so I asked why. She said, "Because when people look at my page I want them to see how many friends I have."

So the answer to the question in the heading above is: sometimes yes, sometimes no. Have fun with your social networking, but don't ever let it replace personal, face-to-face time with your real friends. Because that will always be one of the best things you can do with your time.

Friends are the most important ingredient in the recipe of life.

—Dior Yamasaki

A friend is a gift you give yourself.

—Robert Louis Stevenson

PERSONAL NOTES

Personal Notes

chapter 19 *We all need a purpose that's greater than ourselves*

The purpose of life is a life of purpose.

—*Robert Byrne*

An easy assignment — a challenging assignment

One of the many in-class assignments I enjoyed giving to both my students at the high school and to my adult students at the university had to do with purpose. It was short and simple to assign. For some of my students it was also short and simple to answer. For others it was challenging and time-consuming, and remained in their minds for days. What I enjoyed the most was the discussion that followed the written part of the assignment.

The heading at the top of the assignment page and the instructions were as follows:

A LIFE WITH PURPOSE?

"From ancient times to the present, great philosophers, spiritual leaders, scientists, and scholars have discussed and debated the purpose of life. They don't all give the same explanation, but there *is* a thread of agreement among them.

With that in mind, please answer the following question: What is the main purpose of your life? Explain your answer in one paragraph."

The answers I received always seemed to fall into one of two categories. Here are some samples of the ones I received most frequently:

Category one	Category two
To have fun—party!	To continually learn and grow
To be happy	To help and serve others
To be rich	To contribute something of value
To be somebody (famous)	To live by the teachings of my faith
To be popular	To find a purpose and live it out

Do you see a difference between the answers in the two categories? Do some answers seem shallow? Do some answers have depth of thought? Do some answers appear as if the assignment wasn't taken seriously? Do some answers seem as if the assignment was taken very seriously? Do some answers seem to be about "me"? Do some answers seem to be about "we"? These last two questions are about the main point of this chapter: good people have a purpose that's greater than themselves. This doesn't mean that having fun or being happy, rich, famous, and popular are bad. But it *does* mean that they shouldn't be our sole purpose. There's a much better way to have a life with meaning and joy.

Getting from "me" to "we"

A more fulfilling path is ours for the taking when we find the courage to reach out to others.

—*Craig and Mark Kielburger*
Authors of **Me to We**

We all come into the world with a major flaw: self-centeredness. It's an ugly term that's often associated with some equally ugly terms: conceited, self-absorbed, egotistical, arrogant, superiority complex, narcissistic, self-serving, pride, selfishness, and a "me first" attitude. Have you ever known people with any of these qualities? We all do. Not pleasant to be around, are they? Do any of these terms ever apply to us? Yes—all of us at times, but not to the same degree.

There's a reason why every human being struggles with self-centeredness. Some call it Original Sin, some call it the instinct of self-preservation, and others simply call it human nature. Whatever we call it, everyone is born the same way—infants completely dependent on others for our survival, comfort, affection, and happiness. During this earliest period of our lives we automatically conclude that the world revolves around us. It exists for one reason—to give us what we need and want, and to make us happy. We are the center of the universe.

Some people, sadly, never grow out of this. Even as adults they think that life owes them something, and they can become downright nasty when they don't always get what they want. Others, fortunately, *do* grow out of this "me first" mentality. They realize that life owes them absolutely nothing. In fact, they come to understand that life is a gift, and it's their responsibility to give something back. They move from "me" to "we." And they make the world a better place. Good people have a purpose that's greater than themselves. The more we give, the more we receive. We reap what we sow.

There's no one right way to have a life of purpose. The options are many. The common denominator is "doing good"—being of service to others and to our community, be it worldwide or local. Some people dedicate their entire lives to the service of others. This can be through an international organization, a national crusade, community service, or work through a local place of worship. Some people serve others through their profession. A few examples are social workers, therapists, teachers, people in the medical profession, police officers, fire department workers, and office holders at all levels of government (some of them really are public servants). And some people serve others as private individuals, contributing in a variety of ways.

A related assignment: What are your values?

Your goals and life purpose are grounded in your values.

—*Susan M. Heathfield*

One of the best assignments I was ever given in college had to do with values. I say it was one of the best because it made me think so much, and because it's still part of my everyday thinking more than 50 years later. It took place in Dr. Edward Brusher's Philosophy class when I was a 19-year-old sophomore. He asked us to do something I'd never done before: "Other than God, family, and friends, what are your five highest values?" Panic set in immediately because I wasn't sure what he meant by "values." How could I do the assignment if I didn't know the key word? I assumed I was the only one in the class who didn't know, so I was too embarrassed to reveal my ignorance by asking.

Fortunately, one of the other students saved me by asking, "Dr. Brusher, how are you defining values?" Dr. Brusher said, "Let me put it another way. What are the five things most important to you besides God, family, and friends?" There had to be a reason he left out those three, but I didn't know what it was. And, of course, was too embarrassed to ask because I figured that everyone else understood. But hooray!—yet another classmate came to my rescue. He asked,

"Why do God, family, and friends have to be left out?" Then he added, "Those are my three highest values." Dr. Brusher smiled wisely. He said, "I know that. When I started giving this assignment about 30 years ago, more than 95 percent of the papers turned in had those as numbers one, two, and three. I want you to think about what your other values are."

To this day, I can't remember exactly what I put on that paper. But I do remember writing things down that I thought would look good. Among them were knowledge, wisdom, ethics, and service. Those were words I'd heard from a lot of professors around campus, and I thought they would impress Dr. Brusher. In other words, I was being dishonest— a complete phony. I got my five notable values down, and was feeling pretty smug. Then Dr. Brusher nailed me. He also nailed most of my classmates, because I found out later that they had done the same thing.

He said, "Now write a sentence or two about how you live out each of these values on a day-to-day basis." More panic, and it was much more intense! What was I supposed to write? Those weren't my real values. Had I been honest that day, I would have written basketball, my car, girls, parties, and my clothes. I could have written a lot about how I applied them every day. I learned an important lesson that day: saying what your values are and living by them can be two completely different things.

As the class drew to close, I had hardly written anything. I was starting to sweat. Then Dr. Brusher surprised us all when he said, "I'm not going to collect your papers. I used to, but I got tired of reading so much bullshit (his actual word). All I wanted to do was get you thinking about what's important to you, what kind of life you want to live. Do you want to live a shallow, materialistic, self-centered life, or do you want to contribute something to the betterment of mankind? I suggest that you do this assignment again, but on your own time. You still won't turn it in to me. But you'll get a good start in figuring out what your life purpose is." Then he re-minded us that the values we write down aren't cast in stone. He told us that some of our values change as we acquire new knowledge, meet new people, and have new experiences. He said, "The important thing is to know what your values are, to live by them, and to figure out a life purpose."

Now you can probably better understand why I called this one of the greatest assignments I'd ever been given. I gave it to my high school and college students for many years—exactly the same way Dr. Brusher gave it. It's made a real difference in a lot of peoples' lives. So I'm giving you the same assignment right now, one that you won't turn it in to anyone. What are your highest values? How do you live them out? What is your life purpose?

> I think the purpose of life is to be useful, to be responsible, to be honorable, to be compassionate. It is, after all, to matter: to count, to stand for something, to have made a difference that you lived at all.
>
> —Leo C. Rosten

The real rewards of having a purpose greater than ourselves

While I was writing this book I was also reading one. It's called *Why Good Things Happen to Good People* by Stephen Post, Ph.D. and Jill Neimark. It's one of the most uplifting books I've ever read, and I marked it up furiously. I've quot-ed from it often in my presentations to both kids and adults. The subtitle of the book speaks volumes about the content: "How to live a longer, healthier, happier life by the simple act of giving."

The entire book is based on scientific studies that prove over and over that "being good" is good for us—physically, socially, psychologically, and spiritually. The kinder and more giving we are, the happier and healthier we are. We reap what we sow.

> *I have one simple message to offer and it's this: giving is the most potent force on the planet. Giving is the one kind of love you can count on, because you can always choose it. It's always within your power to give.*
>
> *– Stephen J. Post*

Personal Notes

Personal Notes

---

chapter

20 *The world's best people are always getting better*

Constant development is the law of life.

—Gandhi

A professor's lasting lesson about lifelong learning

I've referred to "pivotal persons" a couple of times earlier in this book. They're those special people who come into our lives and impact us forever. I've also written about "defining moments." They're short periods in time when we see, read, hear, or experience something that changes our perspectives and our lives forever. They often come together. A "pivotal person" can be the source of a "defining moment."

In this case the person was Professor William J. Schwarz, Ph.D., and the moment was in the spring of 1978. Bill, as he preferred to be called, was a professor of education at the University of San Francisco when I was studying for a doctorate. He was everything you could ask for in a teacher: brilliant, well educated (a Ph.D. from Harvard), experienced (he'd previously taught at the University of California), passionately dedicated, and genuinely devoted to helping his students. Just a few minutes after I'd defended my doctoral dissertation (education's most agonizing ordeal) before a scary committee of intellectual giants, Bill asked me to join him in a room across the hall. I think I was still shaking and sweating when he hugged and congratulated me. Then he asked me a curious question: "You know why we put you through all of this academic torture, don't you?" I wasn't sure what he was getting at, but he was smiling, which put me a little at ease. I said, "No, why?" He answered, "So we can show you how much you'll never know. Your education starts today."

I had to think about it for a few seconds, and then I got it. What he was saying is that the more we learn, the more we become aware of how little we know. There's an indescribably vast storehouse of knowledge out there, and even if we went to college for 60 years, we wouldn't even begin to scratch the surface of it. I've never forgotten what Bill said, and more than 30 years later I'm even more aware of how little I know, or ever will know.

Bill and I talked for about a half hour that day, and he said a few other things that I've never forgotten. He said, "I was lucky. I had a wise and highly educated grandmother, and she always encouraged me to learn everything I could, and to never stop. I don't know how many times she said to me, 'The biggest room in the world is the room for improvement.' She said we should never stop learning and never stop improving ourselves in every way we can. She said this is what makes life more challenging, more interesting, more fun, and more rewarding."

Since that conversation many years ago I've become thoroughly convinced that Grandma Schwarz was right. I've also noticed that all the personal heroes I've had throughout life are always working at becoming better. And it's usually not just one thing. These great people work at improving their social skills, growing professionally, practicing their faiths more consistently, learning new skills, and acquiring as much knowledge as they can. This approach to life does, in fact, make life more rewarding.

Lifelong learning and wisdom

*Anyone who stops learning is old, whether at
twenty or eighty. The greatest thing in life is to keep
your mind young.*

—*Henry Ford*

*Wisdom is not a product of schooling but of the
lifelong attempt to acquire it.*

—*Albert Einstein*

Bill Schwarz gave me another priceless gift on the day I completed my doctorate. It was a book recommendation. He suggested that I would appreciate John W. Gardner's 1963 book, *Self-Renewal*. I knew that Gardner was a brilliant man and a devoted public servant, and I had heard of the book, but hadn't read it. I bought it the next day, and devoured it. I still read it often. Gardner's main point is that most people don't reap the rewards life offers. What prevents them from more fulfilling lives is what he calls "stagnation." To stagnate means to not develop or make progress. What holds them back? They stop learning, they stop growing personally. They never acquire wisdom, which Gardner describes as life's greatest prize.

Wisdom and knowledge aren't the same thing. Knowledge is information. Wisdom is applying that information to life. As the dictionary defines it, wisdom is "deep understanding, keen discernment, and a capacity for sound judgment." We can all gain wisdom if we commit ourselves to lifelong learning and personal development—getting better. Wise people know that we get out of life what we put into it. In other words, we reap what we sow.

*Never mistake knowledge for wisdom. One helps
you make a living; the other helps you make a life.*

—*Sandra Carey*

Taking inventory: our strengths and weaknesses

In 1995 I was invited, along with 23 other people, to attend a weekend workshop called "The Balancing Act." I accepted, and it turned out to be one of the most valuable learning experiences I've ever had. How I wished I could have had the same experience in high school, in college, and about every five years throughout adulthood.

The heart of the workshop was actually quite simple. Two weeks before it started we were asked to take a self-inventory on a two-column sheet of paper. On one side was this question: What are your strengths; when are you at your best? On the other side was this question: What are your weaknesses; when are you at your worst? We were asked to give at least five of each, but were free to write more if we wanted.

We were also asked to give a similar sheet of paper to five people who knew us well. They weren't asked to take inventory on themselves, but on us.

On one side it asked, "What do you see as Hal's greatest strengths as a person?" On the other side it asked, "If Hal asked you for some honest and constructive criticism regarding his weaknesses, what would you suggest he work on?" They were filled out by family members, friends, and colleagues. But they weren't given to me. They were mailed in to the workshop people. We got them on the second day.

There was a variety of activities over the three days of the workshop, each one focusing on our six lists of strengths and weaknesses. We all learned that we had some strengths we were unaware of, and we all learned that we had some areas that needed work. By the end of the workshop we each had a list of ways in which we were going to build on our strengths and another list of way in which we were going to improve on our weaknesses.

The main reason this was such a valuable experience is that those six lists of strengths and weaknesses and the list of ways in which I planned to build on strengths and improve on weaknesses are still with me. I wrote them into my journal, and look at them regularly. I'm reminded each time I read them that there's still work to be done. As John Gardner pointed out, we need to renew ourselves on a regular basis.

I'm going to end this final chapter of the book by giving you the same assignment. Here are your instructions:

1. On a separate sheet of paper or in the note pages of this book, make a list of at least five of your strengths and five of your weaknesses.

2. Ask five people who know you well to answer the same two questions my friends and colleagues were asked about strengths and weaknesses, but please give them your name instead of mine.

3. Keep these sheets for the rest of your life. Look at them on a regular basis. And never stop working at getting better.

> *Never stop learning. Never stop improving. It makes life more challenging, more interesting, more fun, and more rewarding.*
>
> —*Rebecca Schwartz*

PERSONAL NOTES

_____

_____

_____

_____

_____

_____

_____

_____

_____

_____

_____

_____

_____

_____

_____

_____

Personal Notes

Summary

This book presents several challenges to be a person of good character. Here's a recap of them:

Develop self-control	Grow from pain and suffering
Have a good attitude	Treat others with love and kindness
Be honest	Achieve through hard work
Feed your mind	Take care of your body
Handle money wisely	Use positive words
Have real heroes	Treasure your friendships
Seek a purpose	Listen to good mentors
Learn to forgive	Always get better

There actually are some people who've mastered all of these character traits. In case you're wondering, the author isn't one of them. He does pretty well at most, but is still working on the others. He's trying to get better, and asks you to join him.

> *Our prayers are answered not when we are given what we ask for, but when we are challenged to be what we can be.*
>
> *—Mortimer Adler*

Conclusion

Almost two thousand years ago St. Paul wrote a letter to his friends in Colossae, a city in the country we now call Turkey. He urged them to practice heartfelt compassion, kindness, humility, gentleness, patience, and forgiveness. Then he added, "And over all of these put on love, that is, the bond of perfection."

What he didn't say was how difficult it would be. It's hard work being a kind and loving person. But it's worth the effort because the result is a life filled with joy. Kindness and love have a way of finding their way back to us. Good things really do happen to people of good character. We reap what we sow.

> *Love and kindness are never wasted. They always make a difference. They bless the one who receives them, and they bless you, the giver.*
>
> —*Barbara De Angelis*

Closing Quotation

If you've read every page of this book, you've read 195 quotations by a wide variety of people from both the past and the present. I love quotations because they seem to have so much wisdom packed in so few words. They also say things more eloquently than the author ever could. I want to end this book with my all-time favorite quotation.

> *Doing nothing for others is the undoing of ourselves. We must purposely be kind and generous, or we miss the best part of existence. The heart which goes out of itself gets large and full. This is the secret of the inner life. We do ourselves the most good doing something for others.*
>
> *—Horace Mann*

I hope that you'll read this quote often, and think about it even more often. Most important, I hope you learn the joy of living by it.

A few words about faith

Faith can be a touchy subject. Millions of people in our country belong to a wide variety of faiths, and millions more are non-believers. Many claim to be spiritual, but not religious. Many claim to believe in a higher power, but not in a personal God. And many others claim that their particular faith is the only true one. Because we have so many different belief systems, I debated long and hard about mentioning my own faith.

It would probably be safer (politically correct) to not write anything about the subject, but because my Christian faith is a central part of my life and writing, I don't want to ignore it. At the same time, it's equally important to say that I have great respect for what all people believe. One of the core teachings of my faith is to not judge or condemn others, so I don't. Another is to treat all people the same way I'd like them to treat me. I try.

> *Don't judge other people and you will not be judged yourselves. Don't condemn and you will not be condemned.*
>
> *—Luke 6:37*

> *Treat other people exactly as you would like to be treated by them—this is the essence of all true religion.*
>
> *—Matthew 7:12*

With the above in mind, this is a book for people of all beliefs. Good character can be developed by any person, regardless of faith, so it isn't necessary to read this as a religious book. Christianity doesn't have a monopoly on either the world's wisdom or its virtues. I cited and quoted teachings from several faiths, even a few non-believers, throughout the book.

At the same time, people who share my Christian faith *can* read this as a faith-based book. You can look in the Bible and find references to every character trait (virtue) mentioned in it. All of us who have faith can use regular reminders that we need to put the teachings of it into practice.

> *Now what use is it, my brothers, for a man*
> *to say he "has faith" if his actions do not*
> *correspond with it?*
>
> —*James 2:14*

Following is one of three verses from the New Testament which I read every morning. Mainly because I need the daily reinforcement to keep me on track. The words in it could apply to anyone.

> *The fruit of the Spirit is love, joy, peace,*
> *patience, kindness, generosity, faithfulness,*
> *gentleness, self-control.*
>
> —*Galatians 5:22-23*

From whatever perspective you read this book, the author hopes it will help you strengthen your character and live a good and meaningful life.

Books by Hal Urban

LIFE'S GREATEST LESSONS
20 Things That Matter
Simon & Schuster, 2003

POSITIVE WORDS POWERFUL RESULTS
Simple Ways to Honor, Affirm, and Celebrate Life
Simon & Schuster, 2004

CHOICES THAT CHANGE LIVES
15 Ways to Find More Purpose, Meaning, and Joy
Simon & Schuster, 2006

THE 10 COMMANDMENTS OF COMMON SENSE
Wisdom from the Scriptures for People of All Beliefs
Simon & Schuster, 2007

The above books are available from the author and anywhere books are sold

LESSONS FROM THE CLASSROOM
20 Things Good Teachers Do
Great Lessons Press, 2008

20 GIFTS OF LIFE
Bringing Out the Best in Our Kids,
Grandkids, and Others We Care About
Great Lessons Press, 2012

Signed copies of these two books can be purchased directly from the author.
They're also on Amazon.com, but at a higher price.

For details visit the author's website: www.halurban.com